HIGH PERFORMANCE CONSULTING SKILLS

The internal consultant's guide
to value-added performance

MARK A THOMAS

THORO*g*OOD

Published 2003, reprinted 2005 by
Thorogood Publishing
10-12 Rivington Street
London EC2A 3DU

Telephone: 020 7749 4748
Fax: 020 7729 6110
Email: info@thorogoodpublishing.co.uk
Web: www.thorogoodpublishing.co.uk

A CIP catalogue record for this book is
available from the British Library.

PB: ISBN 978 1 85418 258 6

Cover and book designed and typeset by
Driftdesign in the UK

Printed and bound in Great Britain by
Marston Book Services Limited, Oxfordshire

Dedication

With love to Jan, Ben and Hannah

Special thanks

Dr Sam Elbeik for his great help and co-operation in originating and developing the terms of reference templates and assistance in the project management area.

Alf Chattel for his continued support and permission in drafting some of the process approaches and methodologies.

May you both continue to thrive and prosper.

Tracey Norbury of HSBC for lending some of her real life observations.

A very special thanks to **Matthias Behrens** of Autodesk for sharing his considerable experience.

Contents

List of illustrations

Introduction

This book will provide you with a highly detailed and practical understanding of the critical client management and handling skills needed to become a high performance internal consultant. The approach and practices I have detailed are based on over 20 years corporate and consulting experience in major blue chip organizations across the globe. Apply them well and you will enjoy extremely successful client relationships.

Internal consultancy brings together a complex range of skills and disciplines and combines them with a distinctive client focus. The purpose in writing this book is to provide you with a daily reference of practical guidance, action points and ideas when managing clients and projects.

With the ever-changing shape of the global economy and organizations it is clear that the internal consultant role is assuming greater importance and is expanding. Since first writing on this trend in 1996 internal consultancy has continued to break into the mainstream of organization life and in particular the role of support functions. If you attend business conferences and read the corporate job advertisements you soon realise that the title 'internal consultant' or 'adviser' is proliferating and now spans all key support functions.

I believe the internal consultancy model offers a major step in harnessing internal knowledge and expertise to improve organizational performance. It is an approach that is very much in tune with the fluid and dynamic nature of today's business world.

I have written with a strong emphasis on the practical 'How to' aspects of internal consultancy. I don't set out to teach you anything about your technical or functional areas of expertise be it information technology, finance, total quality or human resources. My assumption is that you probably already have considerable specialist expertise. What I do set out to do is provide you with a very clear process to manage your clients and projects in a professional and successful manner. I have included many checklists and templates for you to use, adapt or revise to your individual needs.

The emphasis internal consultancy places on moving from a **'colleague to client'** perspective can bring major benefits to both you and any support function you belong to. Indeed the very essence of a client centred consulting relationship involves providing a level of service that exceeds the controlling and bureaucratic tendencies of many traditional support functions. As such the consultancy model has particular relevance if you operate in one of the following roles:

- Information technology and systems specialist
- Finance and internal audit professional
- Human resources or personnel specialist
- Training and development specialist
- Business development specialist
- Project manager
- Administration manager
- Facilities manager
- Customer service and support specialist
- Total quality management specialist

We all know that many organizations continue to outsource support functions with the result that internal customers have the choice to buy external resources. This trend is accelerating in the core support areas of information technology, human resources, training and development and facilities management. Competition is now a daily reality for those of us who work in advisory roles. So, if our support roles are to thrive and prosper in the future organization, we will need to focus relentlessly on providing value added services. The consultancy model offers a major response to these challenges.

At the same time, should you simply want to harness some of the benefits of the operating style of internal consultancy to enhance your existing organizational role, I trust you will find much to meet your needs. As the skills and practices detailed in this book are generic they can be applied to almost any management role in some capacity or other.

I wish you success and many years of successful consultancy work.

Mark A Thomas

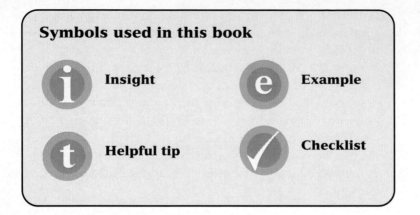

Symbols used in this book

    i   Insight   **e**   Example

    t   Helpful tip   ✓   Checklist

CHAPTER ONE

From managing change to
managing surprise?

ONE
From managing change to managing surprise?

This book is titled *'High Performance Consulting Skills'* and builds on an earlier work *'Supercharge Your Management Role'* that was first published in 1996 and reflected on some of the radical changes taking place in organizations and in particular managerial roles and support functions. Since then those trends have accelerated beyond anyone's imagination.

Between 1998 and 2000 nearly four trillion euros worth of corporate merger transactions were implemented. We have witnessed the traumatic rise and fall of the Dot Coms, along with the rise and collapse of the global telecommunications sector where literally billions of euros appear to have been overspent on securing 3G licences. We are currently experiencing the worst bear market since the Second World War. Added to which we have witnessed some of the most flagrant abuses of corporate power and leadership ever seen at Enron, WorldCom and more recently in Europe with Ahold. All of which has been set against an increasingly insecure and politically unstable world as witnessed by the immense tragedy of September 11th.

It is against this continued volatility and turbulence that organizations are striving more than ever before to achieve new capabilities of flexibility and responsiveness. Organization structures and job roles are in a constant state of flux. Old models of organizing no longer provide tomorrow's growth. Existing concepts of management that rely heavily on notions of planning, checking and controlling are being assigned to the dustbin.

The future is now more uncertain than ever before. In response, organizations are daily announcing major shifts in strategies, product lines and service offerings. Technology is promoting new forms of organization structure and location is becoming less of an issue as to where work is organized and executed. Our old assumptions about how to design, manage and run organizations are subject to constant and radical review. The fact is that we are involved in a period of major upheaval and transition; where simply doing more of what we have done in the past will not sustain us in the future. Today we have to manage by the 'second hand' not the calendar. Increasingly the question is not are we better this year than last, but are we better today than we were yesterday? Equally our planning horizons seem to have to be set in terms of weeks and months rather than years.

So as organizations pursue the benefits of rapid technological change, so to, are new ideas about managing people being explored and implemented. Concepts such as empowerment seek to place greater emphasis on people accepting increased responsibility and control for their work. Such ideas are gaining ground throughout the competitive world. Knowledge management has become one of the buzz-words of the late 90's and early millennium. As a result it is becoming clear that what managers have traditionally practised is being questioned. The classic planning, controlling and reviewing functions of management are being transferred to the people who actually execute the real work. The race to do it 'right first time' means that organizations can no longer afford large numbers of managers controlling people. Self-management is the philosophy and approach that many organizations want to operate in order to win in the competitive world.

Many middle management roles are simply too cumbersome and expensive for organizations to compete against faster and more innovative low cost competitors. The result is a desire to explore new and more radical approaches to the notions of supervision as a means of reducing costs and accelerating competitive capabilities. Many of our existing organizational concepts and practices have had their roots in the 1960's genre of management, so real innovation has been a long time coming.

'The bigger my budget and headcount, the bigger fish I am' philosophy has historically been the basis on which many successful management careers have been built. Indeed such behaviours have been actively encouraged by many organizational reward and appraisal systems. For example, traditional job evaluation techniques have often rewarded jobs that have been characterised by size in terms of the numbers of staff reporting and budget responsibility. But these types of approach have often resulted in management behaviours and practices consisting of internal politicking, empire building and game playing. None of which add value or service to the customer. It is also an approach that results in people becoming overly reliant on their managers to make decisions and take action. In many leading organizations this traditional form of management activity is viewed as redundant. Organizations that possess and promote dependency cultures will not win in the new information and knowledge based era.

In order that organizations can become more innovative, flexible and customer responsive they need to devolve power to the point of customer contact. This requires people to be highly trained and also empowered to take decisions that were previously in the exclusive realm of managers. Thus we enter a new world of organizational working. Where self-directed teams rely on their collective motivation, skills and capabilities to get things done. Rather like the Formula One racing pit team; when it comes to the real work you do not want someone looking over your shoulder to tell you whether you have done it right or not. The reality is that you already know it. At the same time your commitment and skills ensures that for 99.9% of the time you are delivering! Consequently management in the traditional sense becomes an irrelevance. Figure 1 illustrates the transition that is taking place.

YESTERDAY'S PERSPECTIVE	TODAY'S PERSPECTIVE
I am in control	I serve others
I direct and command	I facilitate
People have to come to me	I go to people
I breed dependency	I promote independence
Status and position are important	Status and position are less important than contribution
I think functionally	I think processes
I like clarity and boundaries	I like ambiguity and change

FIGURE 1: THE TRANSITION FROM OLD TO NEW MANAGEMENT

We are therefore witnessing a major shift in the world of work. A shift that is already having immense implications in terms of how we have think about organizations and how they need to be designed and managed.

These changes will however, continue to bring pain as well as opportunities. Many people no longer derive satisfaction from their work. Indeed many managers arrive at their offices and feel under siege from the hundreds of daily e-mails and a 'more and more with less and less' approach.

Some managers are desperately looking for motivation and security in an ever increasingly hostile corporate environment. Given the radical shifts taking place in the corporate world there is little doubt that managers will continue to face immense pressures to reassess their roles. The pressure to increase productivity and demonstrate real added value is relentless. Faced with these challenges the consulting model of operating has the capability to provide hard-pressed managers with a means to move towards a more positive role in the knowledge era.

Support functions under attack

Another aspect of these dramatic changes is that traditional organizational support functions are under severe attack. In the 1990's concepts such as business process re-engineering, with it's emphasis on eradicating non-value added activities resulted in many critical appraisals of conventional support functions such as human resources, finance, internal audit and information technology. This pressure has continued with ever more functions having to make significant changes to their methods of operation. Faced with competitive pressures, organizations are no longer prepared to fund activities that do not add value to the organization, or support the provision of service quality to the customer. Outsourcing has become a global business with lots of major organizations off loading many support activities to a third party. The challenge is simple – 'If you don't add value then you'll have to go!'

When subjected to rigorous analysis and the question 'Why do we do that?' it becomes clear that many aspects of the traditional support function's work do little to support the central nature of the organization. All too often support functions have developed to the stage where they consume large amounts of resource without necessarily contributing to the organization's fundamental goals. In many ways they can be said to have replicated the worst aspects of the old managerial model of controlling and checking and as such they face similar challenges in terms of refocusing their role and contribution. The temptation for any support function is to turn inwards and see itself as the primary customer in organizational relationships. Thus it loses sight of its central purpose and begins to become an end in itself; often growing excessively and engaging in blocking rather than supporting activities to the rest of the organization.

The opportunity

It is against all these fundamental shifts in the world of work and organizations that the increasing use of internal consultants is being observed. Internal consultants achieve results through influence rather than the application of formal executive power. Whilst being aware of the inherent political nature of organizations, internal consultants avoid becoming involved in complex and negative inter-departmental rivalry or politics. By using their specialist technical knowledge, influencing skills and models of organizational change, internal consultants achieve performance improvements. Their method of operating is to enable people to solve organizational problems without the classic need to claim credit for success that for so long has been the driving force of much managerial behaviour. On a strategic level we see internal consultancy providing the following benefits:

- A more flexible and responsive organizational role for managers. Based on contribution not status, and as such in tune with the future direction of the winning organization.

- An overwhelming focus on the delivery of a 'value added' service or contribution; as opposed to controlling and interfering type contributions.

- A relationship that is based on a consultant-client concept rather than a command and control regime.

- A move to process and outcome based thinking. Resulting in the removal of traditional loyalties and hostilities to other functional areas.

What exactly is consultancy?

To define consultancy work is to differentiate it from more conventional forms of management. A consultant's work begins when part of an organization's strategy, structure, processes or systems fail to deliver the necessary levels of performance. Consultants are employed to close the performance gap and their contribution might involve a total solution or the provision of some form of specialist technical support for an agreed period of time. The consultant's involvement in a project can therefore be of a short or long-term nature. The consultant's role is to assist their client without taking over control of the problem. Good consultancy involves providing advice in such a way that it enhances the client's ability to solve their future problems and challenges. You in effect leave something behind – an improved capability. A key reason why the role has so much potential for helping managers operating in flatter structures with empowered workforces.

Invariably a consultant's work also involves the management of change. Whilst having to influence a client and a situation to get things done differently you must achieve this in such a way that your client becomes fully committed to the solution. Being able to influence clients without any formal executive power is one of the defining characteristics of the role. Successful consultants do not rely on overt authority or control to succeed. Instead they rely on their high levels of expertise and influencing skills to persuade people to move to action.

The difference between expert and process consulting

There are two quite distinct types of consulting style and they involve the expert and the process consultant. Both have very different characteristics and methods of working with clients. Figure 2 highlights some of the characteristics and advantages and disadvantages of both types. Most of you reading will be familiar with expert consulting which is typified by the classic external consultant who applies all their knowledge and expertise to diagnose and solve their client's problem in a directive and often prescriptive manner. This form of consulting is very attractive to clients as it can be applied in a very fast and focused way. Information technology for example, has traditionally been an area that has been dominated by expert consulting.

The major difficulty with expert consulting is the lack of client ownership or commitment that results. All too often the recommendations of expert consultants fail at the implementation stage because insufficient emphasis has been placed on developing the client's commitment to the outcomes of the project. Expert consulting involves a directive style and, whilst it is very fast, it does mean that significant issues like client involvement and ownership can be overlooked.

Expert consulting can also prove ineffective in developing the long-term capability of clients. When an expert consultant completes their work they often leave with their expertise so the client is unable to cope with similar problems in the future. Expert consulting can therefore have the effect of breeding organizational dependency on the consultant. Clients are unable to operate without the expertise.

his is of course great news for the consultant but not so good for the client who maybe paying the fees. Process consulting helps to build a client's capability to solve the problem the next time around. To that extent it seeks to promote independence.

PROCESS	EXPERT
Use of all my knowledge and expertise.	Use of all my client's knowledge and expertise
Advantages	**Advantages**
1. Right solution	1. Fast
2. High level of client ownership	2. Focused response
3. Builds client's commitment	3. Right expertise
4. Motivational for the client	4. High impact
5. Promotes client independence and capability	
	Disadvantages
Disadvantages	1. Wrong solution
1. Slow	2. Lack of real understanding
2. May not have right expertise	3. Poor client ownership
	4. No client commitment
	5. Client dependency
	6. Reduces client's sense of confidence

FIGURE 2: EXPERT AND PROCESS CONSULTING

The excessive use of expert consultancy can also lower the morale of a client's organization as it assumes the knowledge and capability to deal with the problem was not within the scope of the client's team. This can be particularly demotivating if the people involved do believe they have the capability to tackle the problems.

In its defence expert consulting does have the benefit of being able to address the right problem with the right expertise.

An organization cannot always be sure that it does have the necessary solution to a problem and so there may well be a need to bring in expertise in very specialist fields to tackle challenging issues. To that extent expert consulting will always have a place in organizations and so remain a credible approach despite its limitations.

e Expert and process consulting

A definition of highly available computing
– The Expert Consultant

'The use of redundant components in conjunction with appropriate fall-over and restart mechanisms in both hardware and software to permit event notification of failure conditions coupled with application and/or database checkpointing and rollback/recover algorithms, thus establishing reasonable assurance within predicted norms that a combination of redundancies will allow a confidence factor to exist and that mean time to repair shall be small enough variable in conjunction with simultaneous mean time between failure of the aforementioned redundant components that the overall system availability will be significantly above normal performance'

Common sense translation – The Process Consultant

'Your computer system should be up and running 24 hours a day, 7 days a week, 365 days a year, so you don't have to be.'

Adapted from an advertisement placed by Data General, Economist November 1994.

In contrast process consulting works on the assumption that a client has the necessary capability to address the problem but needs guidance and advice in the 'how to' of addressing the problem. The emphasis is therefore on helping a client to think through the problem and produce a solution that has a very high degree of commitment and ownership. The major difficulty with process consulting is that it can be much more time consuming than the expert approach. Developing commitment through involvement and discussion is always a longer process, and frequently the urgency of organizational life prevents such time being expended on problem-solving. Quick fix solutions are so often the order of the day.

Process consulting works on the assumption that the client has the necessary expertise to tackle the problem. This of course may not be true. So you may end up wasting a lot of time addressing a problem with the wrong approach or find out that you failed to fully appreciate the problems involved. Whereas the prompt application of some effective form of focused expert consulting would have solved the problem.

Conversely, when it works well, process consulting has the added benefit of enhancing a client's ability to deal with the problem the next time it happens. As such it improves your organization's overall capability. This is something that cannot always be said to be true for expert consulting.

When selecting a form of consulting expertise organizations frequently choose the expert approach because it appears to offer greater benefits in terms of speed and focus. In practice these benefits prove more imaginary than real and much of this book will focus on the process skills that need to accompany any underlying technical expertise. By combining both sets of skills people can develop into truly outstanding internal consultants.

Depending upon your area of functional expertise most internal consultants will need to develop an agility to balance the expert and process continuum. Knowing where to be on this continuum at any one time is the art of a good consultant. External consultants often underestimate the power of process management. They fail to see its power in both developing their client's capability and in generating commitment and ownership to solutions. Hence our general ability to recite horror stories involving external consultants who didn't listen and simply imposed solutions.

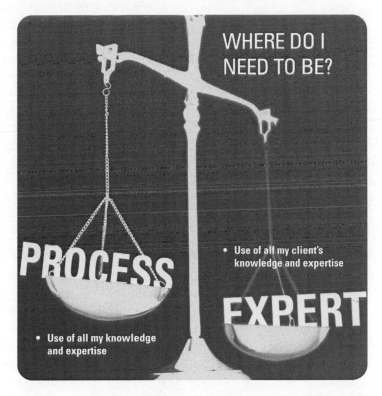

FIGURE 3: WHERE IS YOUR BIAS – EXPERT OR PROCESS?

As an internal consultant, whilst you will apply your technical expertise, whether it be in project management, systems design, training or financial planning, be aware of the constant and potential dangers of assuming that as the expert you know all the answers. Thus forcing your solution onto a client regardless of their own views. Process consulting demands that you focus not only on the problem but also on your client, and you will need to be able to judge the right time to be at either end of this continuum.

The reality of most organizational problems is that there is never one right answer to solve a problem. There are always several options that might be applied. Consequently success in the consulting process involves getting to one of those solutions. More importantly it involves getting your client to the solution that they feel most committed and comfortable with. Achieve this and you are likely to gain immense credibility with your client. Recognising when you need to challenge your clients and when you need to step back are key skills that have to be developed. So learn to balance the expert and process role.

What is the difference between the internal and external consultant?

The classic story of the external consultant who borrows your watch to tell you the time, charges you for it and then keeps the watch, is perhaps a little exaggerated but reality seems to suggest a lot of evidence for the caricature. We are all familiar with the problems associated with external consultants who enter organizations displaying huge amounts of arrogance. Who all too frequently, believe they know what the problem is before even asking any questions. This form of behaviour characterises the worst form of consulting and frequently results in an enormous waste of time, effort and resource. Of course there will always be good and bad external consultants. It also seems likely that there will always be opportunities for good external consultants to thrive. But too often the solution to a problem already exists in an organization way before the arrival of any external consultant.

We have probably all had experience of organizations that are too dysfunctional in the way they are managed to listen to their own people when it comes to diagnosing problems and developing solutions. Despite the prevailing wisdom of some leaders, people who work in organizations do generally know what the problems are. They also understand the underlying issues and have the ideas to fix them. Regretfully, their views and ideas are all too often ignored or dismissed. One of the central themes of this book is to challenge this depressing convention. Indeed it might be argued that it is too often the leadership of an organization where the problem really lies when it comes to encompassing new ideas and approaches.

Internal consultancy provides an exciting and alternative option to these classic but highly frustrating situations. Consultancy is an operating style that aligns itself to the demands of flatter organizational structures and highly skilled knowledge workers.

But in exploring the nature of internal consultancy it is perhaps useful to begin with a comparison with external consultancy as this can help to highlight critical aspects of the role. In examining differences between the two it is not our intention to set one group against another but to simply recognise that there are key differences. As an internal consultant these differences should influence how you ultimately market your services. You will see from the list below that some of the differences can be used to aggressively promote a case for using internal consultancy as opposed to adopting the external route. At the same time there are some issues that will require you to examine and question your own ability to be truly objective and impartial in carrying out internal projects. This question of objectivity is often a major reason why clients may seek external consultancy assistance. In some situations you may well find yourself competing with external consultants for a project. You therefore need to have a clear view of the relative advantages and disadvantages of either approach in order to shape your business case and proposals.

External consultants are:

- **Employed for a fixed period** to work on a specific client problem.

- **Potentially able to get the full attention of senior managers more easily** – clients tend to value more what they have to pay for.

- **Presented as experts** – they have specialist expertise and experience that is not present in the organization. This is often combined with an extensive knowledge of either specific or different industries which clients find very attractive.

- **Generally highly motivated and committed people** who display high levels of energy to their work and clients. And whilst many are paid lots of money for doing this, their motivation and commitment is often to their work and clients first and their pay cheque second.

- **Not always conversant with their client's business**. Thus the client may have to pay for the consultants to learn about their business in the initial stages of a project. This can be expensive.

- **A flexible resource** – the organization is not burdened with long-term costs when the work is finished the consultants leave. Although in some organizations this never seems to happen!!!

- **Able to learn from their clients** and use this learning with other clients.

- **Not emotionally involved in their client's problems** – they have no history of investment in the situation and can therefore be more objective and critical in reviewing situations.

- **Independent** – this is of course debatable – given that someone is going to be signing a bill.

- **Often investing in new approaches and methodologies** – they have to have something new to offer clients.

- **Not always required to live with the consequences of their work.**

- **Not always being entirely honest when they say** 'we've done this!' What they often mean is that 'we haven't but we have really great people and expertise and we are really confident we will find a solution'.

- **Capable of developing a sense of dependency from their clients** – 'we cannot function without you now'.

- **In a business themselves** – they are selling people and time and are interested in consultant utilisation and profit maximisation.

Internal Consultants are:

- **Employed full time** by the organization.

- **Likely to understand the overall business better** than external consultants.

- **Sometimes more knowledgeable that external consultants.** You should know your business and industry extremely well. You may also have developed an approach or methodology that is ahead of any external consultancy group.

- **Normally part of a specific function** – Information Technology, Training and Development, Finance, Business Development, Internal Audit.

- **Aware of the right language and culture of the organization**. You know how things work and how to get things done.

- **Able to identify with the organization and it's ambitions** – as employees you have a big emotional commitment.

- **Liable to being taken for granted** or lacking the credibility of some external consultants.

- **Prone to being too emotionally involved in an organization** – thus perhaps influencing your ability to be truly objective.

- **Required to live with the consequences of their advice** – you are still around long after the external consultants have left.

- **Able to spread their knowledge and experience throughout the organization** – you can enhance your organization's overall capability.

- **Required to redefine past organizational relationships** – the move from 'colleague to client' requires a period of adjustment.

Insight

Working with external consultants

In our experience most external consultants are highly motivated and committed people who want to succeed and deliver high quality work. However because of the negative perception that people in organizations frequently have of external consultants there can be a tendency for people to be hostile towards external consultants. This often results in difficult and strained relationships on joint projects.

If you work with external consultants on a project, seek to work with them and harness their skills and expertise rather than adopting a negative or antagonistic approach. Good external consultants will always respond to positive people and both sides will gain. So get closer. Don't distance yourself, see it as a learning opportunity – but at the same time make sure your positive approach is reciprocated. Don't allow people to simply use you.

So fundamentally internal consultancy promotes the concept of enabling people to develop solutions to their own organizational problems and in so doing develop their long-term capability as well as their organization's. Internal consultancy also provides a basis for managers to propel their existing roles into the organization of tomorrow.

The characteristics of internal consultancy

So what truly characterises being an internal consultant?

Internal consulting is an independent service

Many organizations problems occur because managers become too involved with a problem and so close their minds to certain possibilities or solutions. The need for fresh and independent thinking is one of the main reasons why external consultants are used so often. Although, it is arguable whether external consultants are truly independent. Someone, somewhere is always paying the bill and that can always influence what is reported or recommended. But the ability of internal consultants to provide an independent perspective and analysis is one of their most valued contributions. However, this is an extremely difficult role to play because as an internal consultant you are paid by your organization and as such are part of it. Being critical of something you belong to and which also ensures your financial well-being can be very difficult. You may need to frequently challenge your client on difficult or contentious issues. This may involve confronting managers who are senior in status. In many organizations this can be an extremely challenging task for anyone. Yet providing an independent perspective is an essential requirement of the role. Clients frequently need to have their assumptions and methods questioned. Simply operating as a 'rubber stamp' and confirming a positive image on everything your client is doing may mean failing to carry out an effective consulting role. To challenge the client's objectives, aims and plans is part of the day-to-day role as an effective internal consultant.

Internal Consulting is an advisory service

Internal consultants are not employed to take difficult decisions on behalf of harassed or over-worked managers. As advisors, internal consultants are responsible for the quality and integrity of their advice, but it is their clients who ultimately carry the responsibility for implementation. Providing `advice' in consulting terms can range from a technical input to the provision of counselling or facilitation expertise, but providing the right advice, in the right manner and at the right time is the critical skill of any effective consultant.

For the line manager using the skills of the internal consultant the objective is to empower their team to develop their own solution rather than impose one. The emphasis being to consult and enable not direct and control.

Internal consulting is the application of specialist knowledge, skills and experience

Internal consultants are often employed to work on a problem when part of their organization is either short of specialist skills or lacks the necessary expertise. Depending on your technical background your contribution may involve the introduction of new systems or operational methods. In others the problem may be of a more general nature and involve you operating as a facilitator rather than a technical expert. As a facilitator you are seeking to provide your client with a framework or process to help them solve the problem rather than provide a direct technical or expert input. See the facilitator role as another change from the conventional line perspective which says, 'I will now take over!' Yes, as an internal consultant you have to provide advice and direction but you must stop short of taking over the leadership mantel for the problem.

All internal consultants must keep their knowledge base and expertise up-to-date. The ability to comment or talk about the latest developments in your field of expertise or what is best practice in your industry adds credibility and power to your case. If all we can do as a consultant is talk about a very narrow and limited range of expertise and experience we will find it difficult to get clients to listen to us. Ultimately clients are buying knowledge and advise.

Internal consultancy is a proactive role

In our experience simply changing the title of a department to internal consultancy unit will not result in any immediate overnight transformation. Indeed, if your organization has a negative perception of your department or support function you will need to work hard at changing this image. Simply sitting in your office and waiting for the telephone to ring might (depending on the previous performance of your department) mean waiting for a very long time. Internal consultancy demands a proactive approach with lots of positive networking throughout your organization. The need to explore and identify problem areas and look for opportunities to assist your clients in tackling business challenges is crucial. The need to develop some kind of marketing plan either for yourself or your group as part of this initiative is also vital. Our section on marketing will explore these issues in more depth but being an internal consultant means that you have to start putting yourself around your organization and marketing your services.

Internal consultancy requires a higher business perspective

To become a highly successful internal consultant demands a will to possess or develop an ability to contribute beyond any narrow areas of functional expertise. Whilst traditional organizations have encouraged functional areas of expertise we have all experienced the barriers and hostilities that spring up between functions and departments. Petty conflicts between sales and marketing, research and production are common in all organizations. Any internal consultant or unit, no matter what their area of expertise, must rise above feelings of professional or functional loyalty and display a higher and wider business perspective. Internal consultants need to see themselves as business people first and functional experts second. To contribute to major business issues requires recognition within your organization as an informed person who understands the full business picture and not just a narrow range of technical issues. This again demands a strong sense of personal commitment and development to ensure you keep up-to-date with external issues involving the economy, politics and competitor activity. Clients gain confidence from dealing with consultants they see as knowledgeable and well informed. Narrow perspectives and outlooks do not impress. If you want to get involved in major organizational issues you need to develop a well-rounded outlook on the world in which your organization operates. Be aware of your technical expertise and continually develop it, but do not allow it to become all consuming.

Internal consultancy requires flexibility, personal confidence and credibility

Internal consultancy is a challenging and demanding role. On one level it can involve a very clear and explicit role but on another it has the potential to be an ambiguous role with lots of changing priorities and no clearly defined set of day-to-day tasks. Consequently as an internal consultant the need to be comfortable with a loose role that may mean not knowing what you are going to be doing from one day to another. For some people this can provoke a sense of dis-comfort as they prefer a job that involves a clearly defined set of tasks and responsibilities. But this is not what internal consultancy involves. To operate successfully you have to be comfortable with ambiguous situations and at the same time display a high degree of self-confidence and credibility.

Feeling at ease when working with different groups including senior colleagues and being prepared to challenge and confront them on important issues is vital. This needs to be done without appearing rude, arrogant or patronising. Ultimately your influence and power can only come from the quality of your advice and the manner in which you deliver it. It is not a role for the faint hearted or introverted!

Why use an internal consultant?

In the following section we examine the reasons for employing internal consultants on a project or assignment. We will be working on the assumption that your organization has the capability to establish a consulting unit and that this unit might evolve or develop out of an existing specialist support function role or a more general business development group. Alternatively, if you are going to be operating on an individual basis, you might want to reflect on the reasons why you are being hired as you become involved in projects and other types of internal client work.

Internal consultants can be used for many different reasons so it is important to understand the circumstances surrounding an assignment and to establish why you are being asked to provide assistance. Understanding your client's motives at an early stage can offset problems later on in the working relationship. Your client's motives for employing you can either be positive or negative and in some situations you may have to deal with both. Listed below are some of the classic reasons for using consultants. Look out for the negative uses of consultants as they can be hazardous to your success.

POSITIVE uses of consultants

TO IMPROVE ORGANIZATIONAL EFFICIENCY

Improving organization efficiency is perhaps the most obvious and common reason for using consultants. Organization structure and efficiency reviews involving overhead cost reductions are classic consultancy projects as are those involved with improving operational performance through new management information systems. In the late 1990s we had the widespread use of business process reviews that involved mapping organizational processes in order to streamline core organizational processes. In other situations there may be problems involving customer response times or quality control problems that necessitate a multi-functional response involving systems and training, and development expertise. In all these projects the objective in using consultants is to apply an independent and expert perspective and resource on a difficult and urgent problem.

SUPPLYING AN INTENSIVE AND FOCUSED RESOURCE ON A TEMPORARY BASIS

Major organizational change involving a re-organization or the development of a management information system requires large amounts of senior management time. Day-today operational pressures frequently prevent managers from concentrating exclusively on such tasks. Some senior management teams also find it difficult to focus on both operational and strategic problems at the same time. Management teams often get caught up in other matters or political battles, and progress can be delayed. Internal consultants provide a focused and dedicated resource to assist managers in overcoming these problems. Establishing project teams who focus exclusively on a project or task means that senior management time can be focused and used more effectively.

TO SECURE A CONFIDENT

Some clients like to develop a consultant relationship in order that they can have access to a confident. Being able to listen to a client's problems or issues in a range of disguises can be a much valued role for any internal consultant. In some instances you maybe required to simply listen. To enable your client to express their views on an issue without passing judgement. In others you might be required to challenge or provoke your client's thinking; perhaps to consider alternative approaches or courses of action. This aspect of the internal consultant's role demands that you develop a relationship over a period of time. For clients who do not feel comfortable discussing sensitive issues with their peers or colleagues it can be an extremely valued and powerful role for any internal consultant to perform.

TO CONTRIBUTE TO AN IMPORTANT DECISION-MAKING PROCESS

Where major decisions or projects are involved, managers may want to obtain additional input from consultants to help their decision-making processes. It maybe that research or specialist technical information is required. This involves consultants drawing on their own experience or alternatively obtaining information from other sources, perhaps from outside the organization. It maybe the case that your client is asking you to challenge or test a project or proposal to ensure that every possible issue has been addressed and thought through. Your involvement in such cases is likely to be limited to providing a very focused and technical input for a limited period of time.

TO DEMONSTRATE THAT BUSINESS OPPORTUNITIES ARE BEING IDENTIFIED AND DEVELOPED

Employing consultants on specific business projects is a method by which senior managers can demonstrate that their organization is maximising all the opportunities available to it. Again day-to-day operational pressures sometimes prevent managers devoting the necessary time to explore and examine potential opportunities. Consultants offer the necessary flexibility of resource to enable managers to investigate new ventures.

Conversely some managers who are under pressure or criticism by other colleagues might employ consultants to demonstrate that they have a difficult situation under control. Clearly this action might be interpreted as a negative use of consultants because it can involve them in complex and potentially hazardous organizational politics.

TO REDUCE THE RISK OF A PROJECT'S FAILURE

Where highly complex and expensive projects are concerned the involvement of consultants with high-level expertise can obviously reduce the risk of a project running into difficulties. Employing specialist expertise or project management skills provided by consultants helps provide comfort to senior managers that an important project is being properly resourced, supported and managed. As well as providing the expertise you may be acting as a comfort blanket to the organization.

Potentially NEGATIVE uses of consultants

Of course there are those instances where consultants can be used for negative or even subversive reasons or purposes. In such cases you need to be extremely cautious of getting involved as the potential outcomes of these situations can have negative implications for your credibility and reputation. When this happens your ability to operate successfully in your organization becomes seriously impaired.

TO HELP UNDERMINE AN EXISTING MANAGEMENT GROUP OR SITUATION

In some situations a consultant might be employed to deliberately attack a specific proposal or initiative that has been sponsored by another manager or group. This can involve you in an acrimonious relationship and a 'no win' situation. There is a distinct difference between situations where you might be asked to critically evaluate or validate a proposal or action plan, and those where there is a hidden political agenda that is not explained to you at the outset of a project. You should always probe to establish the reasons why your client has decided to involve you. If your suspicions are aroused probe harder to uncover the real motives.

If you suspect or sense a difficult situation you will need to explain to your prospective client your concerns. You need to point out the potential dilemmas you face in trying to operate successfully in the long-term if you become involved in such a project. Always remember that if you are seen as someone who does the 'dirty work' of others you will have problems when next trying to operate in other parts of your organization.

PROVIDING MANAGEMENT WITH SUPPORT TO JUSTIFY PREVIOUSLY AGREED DECISIONS OR ACTIONS

In certain situations, internal consultants maybe asked to tackle assignments in order that a manager can justify an already agreed course of action by reference to a consultant's report or recommendation. This is not an unreasonable request, but as a matter of principle, and in your own self-interest, you should try to avoid such projects. Internal consultants must always safeguard their reputation and independence. Accepting work of this nature can influence peoples' views on your integrity. If you lose your integrity then your ability to operate successfully in the future will be seriously impaired. People who are suspicious of your motives and behaviours are unlikely to co-operate with you in providing information and assistance. As an internal consultant avoid overtly 'political' assignments.

TO HAVE SOMEONE TO BLAME

Whilst we have advocated the use of consultants on important projects it is also the case that in some extreme situations certain managers will view the involvement of consultants as providing them with a convenient scapegoat in the event that a project does not produce a satisfactory outcome. In such situations it is critical that you secure your client's agreement to all stages of a project and that you manage their commitment throughout the project so as to avoid criticism at a later stage. If you sense the situation is one where you will be unable to emerge without damage you should avoid entering the project at the outset.

Managers might also use internal consultants to recommend or implement particularly difficult actions such as staff reductions or business closures. The tactic can involve hiding behind the consultant's recommendations so as to push through the difficult process in the hope that the reputation of management is not diminished. Suffice to say, people often see through the tactic with the result that a management's reputation is often further damaged rather than enhanced.

However, there maybe some legitimate reasons whereby a client might legitimately employ this tactic for some longer-term benefit that might not be immediately apparent. There are circumstances involving complex re-organizations and key staff deployments where it maybe acceptable for a manager to refer to a consultant's recommendation. In such situations, the manager may have in mind the stability of future working relationships and the need for the consultant to be fully recognised as the agent of the changes. Indeed it can be argued that this method of using consultants is the act of a skilled and thoughtful manager trying to take a long-term and beneficial outlook on a difficult problem.

Clearly none of these situations are easy to cope with or manage, so you need to carefully weigh up the potential benefits and losses involved and discuss these with your potential client before becoming involved in such projects.

How to become an internal consultant

The Manager

The skills contained in this book are highly relevant to any manager in a modern organization. The move from traditional command and control structures to more empowered working practices, means that managers are increasingly becoming enablers or facilitators to their people. The new role provides a means of support that allows people to develop and improve organizational performance without the necessity to feel dependent on conventional management powers. Consultancy skills, and in particular the process skills involved in handling client relationships, can be employed not just on projects but also in day-to-day working relationships between managers and their people. The consultancy model provides a viable means by which traditional managers can start to change their operating mode to the modern world.

The Support Function

Any support function can become an internal consultancy unit by merely possessing or having developed a body of knowledge, experience and skills in managing specialist activities or tackling difficult technical problems. However, experience indicates that there also needs to be an underlying organizational move towards developing an internal consulting capability. Such changes need to be accompanied by a clear communications strategy which sets out the rationale for introducing the role and the implications for managers, and their working relationship with the new support function. It is not sufficient to simply change the role without communicating and educating managers about the new regime. Managers who have been used to a traditional form of support function will need to understand the new changes in service provision.

Some organizations that are aggressively pursuing the consulting concept, have gone as far as to introduce new financial procedures which require line managers to contract with the consultancy unit for a project or assignment fee. Other organizations have changed the operating role without altering the funding or resourcing requirements. In either situation senior managers and those employed in the consultancy unit will need to ensure that they have communicated thoroughly with the rest of the organization. Failure to do so will invariably result in confusion and managers complaining about the new service provision. Any line manager, who for fifteen years has picked up their telephone to their personnel or IT department and received an immediate response, will react angrily the first day they are told that it will be a week before you can meet them. You have to clearly inform managers about the new role. It is a communications process that cannot be left to chance and must involve a high level dialogue with all managers throughout your organization.

Time to convert and redirect

Embarking on this approach also demands time and patience. In most organizations it is not possible to simply close down one day and start operating as a consultancy unit the next. Invariably managers and functions require a period of adjustment. Time is needed to convert from the old to the new, as is the recognition that there will be tensions in making the transition. These changes require careful planning as you and former customers need to adjust to a new working relationship.

In addition to possessing functional or specialist expertise, consulting skills also requires the ability to collect and analyse information, to develop options, and recommend practical and workable solutions and action plans. The need to keep pace with the latest developments, methodologies and techniques in your specialist field of expertise is vital. The continuous development of skills and knowledge base is a critical means by which to achieving credibility and influence with clients. It is only over a gradual period of time that anyone can expect to make the transition and people need to be realistic about the time this will take.

CHAPTER **TWO**

The art of client management

TWO
The art of client management

Understanding the key stages of the internal consulting process

In this chapter we outline the key stages and activities involved in managing successful projects. Our consulting process involves a systematic approach to managing projects or assignments. This ensures you not only deliver successful results but also enjoy strong and positive client relationships. The skills involved in managing projects can also be applied in lots of day-to-day working relationships in the corporate world. Making a successful transition from colleague to client requires the careful application of these consulting stages.

A consultancy project or assignment can be divided into four key stages that run throughout the duration of a project. These stages are shown in Figure 4 and involve:

1 Getting in and contracting with your client

2 Information gathering – understanding the client's problem

3 Presenting client feedback and action planning

4 Implementing, reviewing and exiting the project

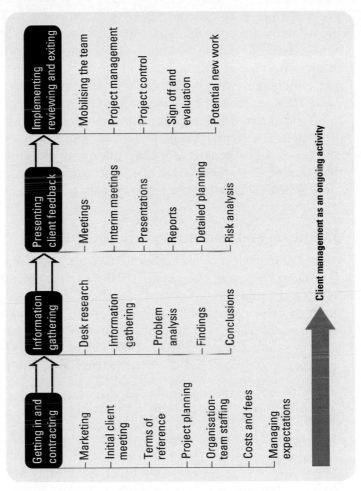

FIGURE 4: THE CLIENT MANAGEMENT PROCESS

As an internal consultant it is likely that in most cases you will be expected to get involved in all of these four stages. However, it is important to remember that on some assignments, your participation in the implementation phase might be reduced as your client decides to take on these responsibilities.

No two projects or assignments are ever the same and so we need to remain flexible and responsive to a client's specific needs and demands. Some clients will want to rely heavily on your services throughout the duration of a project. Others may want to reduce their dependency on you by absorbing much of the work involved in any action planning and implementation phases. As an internal consultant you need to be comfortable with both arrangements. Don't feel personally rejected if your client decides to reduce your involvement in this latter stage of a project, unless of course you have done something negative to justify your exclusion!

Getting in and contracting with your client

As an internal consultant you have to have a group of potential clients who recognise your expertise and are willing to involve you in projects or initiatives when suitable opportunities arise. Your ability to generate interest in your services is the first step to obtaining an invitation to meet with any potential clients. To succeed in this area you will have to market yourself and, where appropriate, your team or unit's services.

MARKETING INTERNAL CONSULTANCY

For the new or inexperienced consultant the prospect of having to go out into their organization and actively market or sell their services can come as a shock, but the fact is internal consultancy demands this approach. Indeed, if we think about it, everyone in the corporate world is in the business of selling. If your organization is unaware of who you are and what you can offer, the chances of you being asked to discuss problems and provide advice to clients will be remote. If you cannot rely on potential clients coming to you then marketing your services becomes essential to your survival. Developing a marketing approach represents a significant departure to the work of many traditional managers and support functions that have enjoyed a captive market for their services. To some it comes as a bit of a shock. Often the fear of selling in a competitive world puts many people off becoming independent external consultants. But the fact is that in today's environment we have to think about how we market ourselves and capabilities.

In our chapter on marketing we outline some of the specific actions needed to begin the marketing process in your organization. These include developing a simple marketing strategy and promoting your skills and services to senior management and other key stakeholder groups in the organization.

When your initial marketing efforts have been successful, a potential client will invite you to a meeting to discuss a particular issue or problem and to explore whether you might be able to provide some help. This is your selling opportunity and for most internal consultants the probability is that you will have worked for this person before. However, to succeed as an internal consultant you need to manage this person in a very different way to the past. This is where we need to start developing a very structured approach to managing client relationships.

INITIAL CLIENT MEETINGS

Initial client meetings represent the formal start of our client management process. It also begins the move from a colleague to client perspective in the working relationship.

The purpose of any initial client meeting is to begin understanding the client's business and problems. This involves jointly exploring their key challenges and concerns and establishing the possible basis for a project or assignment. At this initial stage you need to be prepared to start discussing provisional objectives, and timescales. You might also raise the possible involvement of the client's staff in the work and any requirements for specialist skills such as finance, human resources, project management, production, engineering, logistics, information technology, etc. Clearly this requires some advance preparation and so is a very different approach to the colleague perspective of ' I'll just turn up and see what they have to say!'

As a new internal consultant there is often a real need to redefine past relationships with some of your clients. Clients may have viewed you past role as that of a subservient support function. If you are going to gain the respect and authority you need, you will have to shift any negative perceptions. It is critical that clients view you as an equal. As an internal consultant you want to have a strong and mutually respectful relationship with all your clients. In effect you have to develop a partnership relationship. But depending on your starting point this may take time. Patience will be needed in order to build up a range of positive successes to shift peoples' attitudes. This process of influencing your clients' perceptions and attitudes begins at the initial meeting stage.

DEVELOPING AN INITIAL TERMS OF REFERENCE

On the basis that both you and your client have had a satisfactory meeting and agreed in principle to start working together, an initial terms of reference has to be developed. Once submitted this draft document can be discussed and possibly agreed at your next client meeting. In many situations you may need to carry out some preliminary research to define the precise scope of the problem although for some simple and straightforward assignments it maybe possible to agree the initial terms of reference at your initial client meeting.

Agreeing an initial terms of reference with your client before you begin any consulting work is a fundamental rule in managing all of your client relationships. The consultant and client must be absolutely clear about the scope and objectives of a project at the beginning. The process of agreeing an initial terms of reference ensures that a clear and mutual understanding has taken place. Many consultants have met with failure and ultimately faced an angry client because they ignored this basic rule. Assuming that a lack of clarity in understanding at the start of a project will not matter in the final stages of a project, is a fatal mistake. The fact is it matters a great deal. Clients and consultants can easily misunderstand or forget the details of initial discussions. This can be further exacerbated if any agreements are not documented. Establishing an initial written terms of reference is the means by which you establish a clear focus on what your client wants and agrees to. It is also a process that helps develop your client's thinking about their problem and what it is they exactly want from you. Very often a client's view of a problem can change significantly as a result of a consultant probing and challenging them at an initial meeting. So the process is intended to benefit both parties by ensuring that there is a clear understanding of the aims of a project. This helps prevent any surprises later on in a project.

> Don't start work without a terms of reference – it's a powerful a tool to help surface competing stakeholder objectives and deliverables. It really helps the client focus on questions such as, 'Do we really want to do this?' and 'What are we hoping to achieve?'
>
> *Tracey Norbury, Internal Training Advisor HSBC*

As a project develops constantly review your terms of reference. When circumstances surrounding a project change you may well need to adjust the overall objectives. This is why we refer to an 'initial' terms of reference at the beginning of a project as it is very likely that it will change, especially where you become involved in complex implementation work that will require detailed planning schedules.

In developing your initial terms of reference you should include the following information:

- Background to the project.
- Project's objectives.
- Boundary of the project.
- Constraints involved.
- Assumptions you are making at this stage.
- Client's reporting requirements.
- Project deliverables and milestones.
- Show who and when things happen on an Activity Time chart (Gantt).
- Finance/resources required to carry out the project.

In most cases, to fully understand your client's problem, you will need to complete a brief but intensive period of fact finding. This may involve you interviewing a small cross section of people or conducting some form of desk research. Make sure that you understand the background to your client's problems so that you can provide an initial estimate of the resources and time you will need to complete the project. When your terms of reference are agreed with your client they in effect become your consulting contract. They also become the basis on which your eventual success or failure will be judged which is why they assume such significance in the client management process. Without a clearly agreed terms of reference you cannot hope to deliver effective consulting services.

Insight

Never lose focus of your terms of reference and keep them readily available throughout the course of any project. On complex or lengthy assignments it is very easy to lose sight of your original objectives and stray from your terms of reference. This can be very damaging either towards the end of an assignment or when you have to report back at key stages. You do not want your client to feel you have not delivered so keep asking yourself and your colleagues 'Have we done what we said we would do?'

On some projects, you will be required to bid for the work and compete with other groups, possibly external consultants. Preparing an initial terms of reference will not be enough as you will have to prepare a client proposal. This is a formal document that will include your initial terms of reference as well as:

- your consulting experience – document your experience and skills and that of the team; and

- methodology – describe your approach to executing the work.

Insight

Consultants always leave insufficient time for drafting and producing client reports. A useful guide in planning is to simply double the time you think you will need! You can never do enough drafting and editing of a final report.

Information gathering and understanding your client's problem

In the majority of assignments or projects, a detailed period of fact finding will be necessary to ensure that you are obtaining the right information to understand and accurately define your client's problem. This requires an inquisitive and open-minded approach throughout your investigation. Simply accepting what is said to you without challenging or questioning the issues may result in you developing erroneous findings and conclusions. A structured and analytical approach is needed to ensure that all the relevant facts and issues are established and understood. Having a clear understanding of the information gathered during the initial stages of your work, will also help you highlight additional areas which may require further investigation. Ultimately you must be able to develop valid conclusions and recommendations from all the gathered facts.

The main methods of gathering information are:

- Desk research that typically involves the review and examination of existing information or records (e.g. current reports, efficiency statistics, systems outputs, policies, operating procedures and sales or customer data, etc.).

- Interviews conducted on an individual basis.

- Group interviews.

- Questionnaires circulated to staff, customers, suppliers or other relevant parties.

- Process mapping of existing processes or systems.

- External case studies or data sources.

Most consultancy projects will involve a combination of all these methods. Interviews are of course always critical in gathering information and it is impossible to carry out consulting work without having to interview people. When conducting client interviews always aim to:

- Be professional, respectful and courteous to everyone.

- Have a checklist of the main questions and issues you want to discuss.

- Challenge and be a devil's advocate if some answers seem not to make sense.

- Remain impartial (never criticise client staff or others within the organization and never be drawn into making controversial statements).

- Distinguish clearly between information that is given to you 'on the record' and 'off the record'.

- Be discrete.

To be successful interviews need to be conducted in a relaxed and open atmosphere. There may also be moments when you need to maintain client confidentiality with regard to personal 'off the record' comments. You may need to protect people who share confidential information with you by giving assurances that you are only identifying broad themes and issues rather than attributing specific comments to individuals. Giving the impression that whatever is said will be quickly passed on to all interested parties is not likely to generate an atmosphere of trust.

CONTROLLING THE PROJECT

Once your project gets under way, your main responsibility is to ensure that the plan is implemented so that the objectives in your terms of reference are met. You have to therefore constantly focus on your project's objectives by:

- tracking the team's progress against the plan; and

- reviewing the plan to ensure that it remains current and viable.

Keeping track of your project against schedule is a key consulting discipline. The need to ensure that people are aware of their key targets and deliverables is vital. As is the need to maintain a strong level of communication across all aspects of the project team and the activities they are undertaking. People need to be aware of the bigger picture and it is the role of the project manager to ensure that people are kept up-to-date on developments and progress. Early warning mechanisms need to be in place in the event that delays or problems occur. So strict adherence to any project plan is vital to success.

Successful projects are best achieved by holding regular review meetings and ensuring that all key decisions are fully documented. Agreed action points should be circulated to everyone involved in the project. Structured client progress meetings also ensure your client is kept fully informed of the work being undertaken, and of the project's overall progress and development. It also means you can highlight any problem areas at an early stage. It is vital that you keep your client involved at all times, so as to manage the client's commitment throughout the implementation phase.

Finally, re-planning may need to take place after holding a review meeting. You need to record any new or changed tasks and also change your terms of reference if appropriate. In some cases there maybe no need to revise your plan.

Alternatively, you may have to consider a number of management actions, such as increasing resources, reassigning people and tasks before rescheduling parts of your project in order to keep to the planned deliverables.

Presenting client feedback

Presenting client feedback is a phase of the consulting process that runs throughout the life-cycle of any project or assignment you are involved with. Client feedback has to take place regularly during any project to ensure that your client is kept up-to-date on progress and advised of any difficulties at an earlier, rather than later, stage. Any consultant who neglects this part of the consulting cycle is likely to run into real problems with regard to the client relationship. Remember to always take the initiative when communicating with your client. Never be in the position where your client is chasing you for information or progress updates. If you find yourself in such a situation it probably means that you have failed to pay sufficient attention to the feedback process in the client relationship. When it comes to feedback and progress reports, always stay one step ahead of your client. Never, ever, try to hide problems or delay giving bad news as it always makes the situation worse. Better to advise your client today rather than three weeks after a problem has occurred. The chances are that the problem will be and sound a lot worse in three weeks time.

Any project completion date ultimately results in some form of final report or client presentation. During this stage of the feedback process your client is looking to assess the quality and integrity of your work, and you in turn are looking to gauge their reactions. It is also the stage at which you will be aiming to further strengthen your client relationship by securing agreement to your findings, conclusions and recommendations.

The two major activities involved in presenting client feedback will involve you in writing reports and making formal presentations. They constitute two critical skill areas that must be mastered. Poor performances in either can seriously damage your client's confidence in your overall ability and competence.

WRITING CLIENT REPORTS

Any client report must be a clear statement of what you set out to do, what you did, your recommendations and where appropriate your proposed implementation plans. As an internal consultant, your report must be capable of being understood at a first reading by anyone who does not possess a detailed knowledge of the problem or issues under review.

Report writing is a complex and at times painful process but there is no escaping from the discipline that must be applied. All consultants experience difficulty at one time or another in writing reports, so you should not be too depressed when you find yourself struggling with a complex report. But you must recognise that there is a significant difference in the skills needed to analyse a complex problem and to then write a clear and logical report on the situation. However, both sets of skills are necessary to produce a report that is rigorous in analysis and clear in presentation. In many projects your final report is often the only way in which your client can, or will, judge your performance, so you have to display a high degree of skill and capability.

MAKING CLIENT PRESENTATIONS

Whilst your conclusions and recommendations should always be discussed with your client in advance of your final report being submitted, there invariably comes a time when you will be expected to make a formal presentation on your work.

Client presentations are one of the most important parts of an internal consultant's work. During the latter stages of a project they become critical as they provide you with the opportunity to explain issues in your report that might not be immediately clear and open to misinterpretation. When working on sensitive projects you should always personally present your report rather than send it to your client. This allows you to clarify any potentially contentious or difficult issues immediately. Following any client presentation, you may need to consider reviewing and possibly amending your final report in the light of the comments received during your presentation.

Like report writing client presentations can be extremely complex events and you can never plan or prepare enough for them. During any presentation you may have to deal with sensitive issues involving criticism of your client or other managers or departments. You may also have to safeguard confidential issues that emerged during your work. When issues such as these are present, you need to not only plan for them, but also how you will manage them during the actual presentation. As such you will need to be skilled in not only structuring presentations but also in planning around detailed process issues. For example, how to deal with the fact that attending your presentation might be two managers who you know to be extremely hostile to what you have to report? Dealing with this type of issue is an everyday challenge for the internal consultant. In our client presentation section we will outline some of the techniques that you can use to ensure that you manage such situations and secure your client's support and commitment at the feedback stage.

Implementation

Implementation is that stage of the consulting process that requires detailed plans for achieving the project's objectives. On some projects your involvement may end at this stage with your client taking over control. If your involvement in a project does end at this stage you must be aware that as far as your client is concerned the project is not finished. The completion of your review or the delivery of a report, frequently represents a beginning not an end for the client.

On very large and complex projects involving, for example, a major information systems implementation, your client will frequently have to manage a large workload and it maybe necessary to involve a specialist project manager to carry out the detailed planning and monitoring activities. In such situations large numbers of people and resources will be involved and this demands a more disciplined and rigorous approach to project management. However, in the majority of consulting projects, the responsibility for carrying out the detailed planning and implementation management will lay with you as the internal consultant in charge of the project. So you have to be prepared to take on the role and develop some of the skills of a project manager.

Insight

Identify and involve all the appropriate people who will participate in the planning discussions. These are the people who will ultimately assume responsibility for any new systems or procedures and so their active involvement must be secured. As a minimum, these people will include your client, their management team and any other key people who will implement the system or changes.

The implementation phase involves the following steps:

- Assessing how much detailed planning you need to do.
- Reaffirming your terms of reference.
- Preparing a quick work programme.
- Carrying out a quick risk analysis.
- Presenting your plan to your client.
- Secure your client acceptance to the plan.

Reviewing and exiting projects

At the end of a project you will need to assess whether or not a successful outcome has been delivered and you have met the objectives set out in your original terms of reference. The most appropriate way to do this is to present your client with a review report of your project work and the final results. This review process can also involve identifying additional or further actions that might be required to achieve a project's final objectives. It might, in some circumstances, identify who should undertake any additional work and specify the timescales involved. The review process should always be undertaken in partnership with your client. This approach is a positive sign that shows the project was conducted in a mature and professional manner where both the client and consultant accepted their responsibilities for the outcome.

As a successful internal consultant your time will be at a premium. With many clients requesting your services, you will have to manage their expectations with regard to your future availability. If you allow your clients to believe that they have endless freedom to demand your services at any time, you will never be able to operate successfully. So, at the end of an assignment, you must inform your client that the project and your involvement has come to an end and that any additional work will have to be subject to a new agreement.

Project management – people and team management

The other major component in managing client projects involves the process of building, managing and leading teams. When it comes to people and relationships we enter a very different arena to that which involves defining critical paths and conducting risk and probability assessments. Applying project management tools and techniques is one thing, managing people is another. As we all know, managing people in the working environment for the most part involves a complex world where emotions such as ambition, motivation, competition, power, control, co-operation, trust and mistrust come into play.

Clearly no client assignment or project can be managed without the need to manage relationships. These will normally involve your project sponsor, their staff, stakeholders and your project team. Altogether this group presents a very challenging aspect of the internal consultant's role. Fail to manage people and we fail to manage projects. So for the vast majority of internal consultants, managing the client element is often the most demanding aspect of the role. In any project situation our people management experiences will almost certainly vary from one project to another, but the essential factors that we will need to cope with include:

- Managing the day-to-day client relationship – managing expectations, communicating progress and liasing on problem areas.

- Defining your project leadership role and style – deciding on the right amount of task control and relationship support provided to the team. Bringing out the best of individual talents and getting people to work towards a common goal.

- Managing the various group dynamics – this includes the roles and relationships between the various team members and other interested parties. In other words building the team.

SELECTING THE PROJECT TEAM

Based on the project you are undertaking you need to select the right balance of skills and competences. As well as considering the technical skills required, you will also need to think about the balance of your team in terms of personalities and basic project management disciplines. In such cases it might be helpful to consider using some form of team building instrument to help get the team started. Meredith Belbin's approach to team preferences is an excellent way to kick-off a project team and get people understanding the roles they might play in helping to build an effective team.

The benefit of Belbin's work is that it provides not only the project manager but also team members with a clear means of understanding the following:

- Our own individual contribution to the team.

- How other team members contribute.

- How best to allocate activities and tasks amongst the team.

- Where gaps in the team composition might exist and how best to manage them.

Figure 5 (overleaf) shows the eight classic types identified.

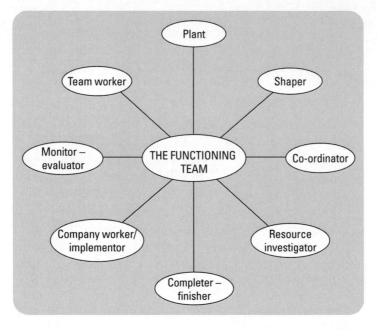

FIGURE 5: BELBIN'S TEAM TYPES

Once we understand our own team roles and their strengths and weaknesses as defined by Belbin, we have a mechanism by which we can, as internal consultants and project leaders, improve the balance of our teams and their overall effectiveness.

Belbin's team roles – questionnaire

Directions for completing the questionnaire:

For each section allocate a total of ten points among the sentences that you think best reflect or describe your behaviour. The points you allocate may be distributed among several sentences: in extreme cases they might be distributed among all the sentences or ten points may be given to a single sentence.

After having worked through the questionnaire enter your points into the table at the end. Then add up the scores vertically to obtain your scores for each of Belbin's types.

1 What I believe I can contribute to a team:

a) I think I can quickly see and take advantage of new opportunities. ☐

b) I can work well with a very wide range of people. ☐

c) Producing ideas is one of my natural assets. ☐

d) My ability rests in being able to draw people out whenever I detect they may have something of value to contribute to group objectives. ☐

e) My capacity to follow through has much to do with my personal effectiveness. ☐

f) I am ready to face temporary unpopularity if it leads to worthwhile results in the end. ☐

g) I am quick to sense what is likely to work in a situation with which I am familiar. ☐

h) I can offer a reasoned case for alternative courses of action without introducing bias or prejudice. ☐

2 If I have a possible shortcoming in team work it could be that:

a) I am not at ease unless meetings are well structured, controlled and generally well conducted. ☐

b) I am inclined to be too generous towards others who have a valid viewpoint that has not been given a proper hearing. ☐

c) I have a tendency to talk a lot once the group gets onto new ideas. ☐

d) My objective outlook makes it difficult for me to join in readily and enthusiastically with colleagues. □

e) I am sometimes seen as forceful and authoritarian if there is need to get something done. □

f) I find it difficult to lead from the front, perhaps because I am over-responsive to the group atmosphere. □

g) I am inclined to get too caught up in ideas that occur to me and so lose track of what is happening. □

h) My colleagues tend to see me as worrying unnecessarily over detail and the possibility that things may go wrong. □

3 When involved in a project with other people:

a) I have an aptitude for influencing people without pressurising them. □

b) My general vigilance prevents careless mistakes and omissions being made. □

c) I am ready to press for action to make sure that meetings do not waste time or lose sight of the main objectives. □

d) I can be counted on to produce something original. □

e) I am always ready to back a good suggestion in the common interest. □

f) I am keen to look for the latest in new ideas and developments. □

g) I believe others appreciate my capacity for cool judgement. □

h) I can be relied upon to see that all essential work is organized. □

4 My characteristic approach to group work is that:

a) I have a quiet interest in getting to know colleagues better.

b) I am not reluctant to challenge the views of others or to hold a minority view myself.

c) I can usually find a line of argument to refute unsound propositions.

d) I think I have a talent for making things work once a plan has to be put into operation.

e) I have a tendency to avoid the obvious and come out with the unexpected.

f) I bring a touch of perfectionism to any team job I undertake.

g) I am ready to make contacts outside the group itself.

h) While I am interested in all views, I have no hesitation in making up my mind once a decision has to be made.

5 I gain satisfaction in a job because:

a) I enjoy analysing situations and weighing up all the possible choices.

b) I am interested in finding practical solutions to any problems.

c) I like to feel that I am fostering good working relationships.

d) I can exert a strong influence on decisions.

e) I can meet people who may have something new to offer.

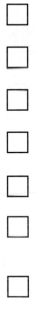

f) I can get people to agree on a new course of action. ☐

g) I feel in my element where I can give a task my full attention. ☐

h) I like to find a field that stretches my imagination. ☐

6 If I am suddenly given a difficult task with limited time and unfamiliar people:

a) I would feel like retiring to a corner to devise a way out of the impasse before developing a line. ☐

b) I would be ready to work with the person who showed the most positive approach however difficult they may be. ☐

c) I would find some way of reducing the size of the task by establishing what different individuals might best contribute. ☐

d) My natural sense of urgency would help to ensure that we did not fall behind schedule. ☐

e) I believe I would keep cool and maintain my capacity to think straight. ☐

f) I would retain a steadiness of purpose in spite of the pressures. ☐

g) I would be prepared to take a positive lead if I felt the group was making no progress. ☐

h) I would open discussions with a view to stimulating new thoughts and getting something moving. ☐

7 With reference to the problems to which I am subject to in working in groups:

a) I am apt to show my impatience with those who are obstructing progress. ☐

b) Others may criticise me for being too analytical and insufficiently intuitive. ☐

c) My desire to ensure that work is properly done can hold up proceedings. ☐

d) I tend to get bored rather easily and rely on one or two stimulating members to motivate and stimulate me. ☐

e) I find it difficult to get started unless the goals are clear. ☐

f) I am sometimes poor at explaining and clarifying complex points that occur to me. ☐

g) I am conscious of demanding from others the things I cannot do myself. ☐

h) I hesitate to get my points across when I run up against real opposition. ☐

Interpretation of Scores

Allocate the scores from the above questions into the table below. Then add up the points in each column to give a total team-role distribution score.

Section	CW	CH	SH	PL	RI	ME	TW	CF
1	g	d	f	c	a	h	b	e
2	a	b	e	g	c	d	f	h
3	h	a	c	d	f	g	e	b
4	d	h	b	e	g	c	a	f
5	b	f	d	h	e	a	c	g
6	f	c	g	a	h	e	b	d
7	e	g	a	f	d	b	h	c
Total								

Source: With permission from Dr Meredith Belbin 'Management Games' and publishers Butterworth Heinemann

Belbin originally identified eight types or preference for working in teams. More recently Belbin has updated his work and revised some of the names allocated to types. The Chairman has become the Co-ordinator whilst the Company Worker has become the Implementor. At the same time a new type has been introduced. The Specialist is someone who provides a very strong but narrow input; Specialists are good at providing specialist information and facts. They may not be so good at relating to other team members or detracting themselves from the narrow functional or specialist role. For the purpose of this work we have used the former profiles adopted by Dr Belbin and simply highlighted the name changes that he has introduced. Readers wishing to familiarise themselves more with his work should review his books published by Butterworth Heinemann and in particular *Team Roles at Work* as they provide a more detailed explanation of his research and findings.

Listed below are some of the essential characteristics of each type:

- Company worker/implementor   – CW
- Chair/co-ordinator   – CH
- Shaper   – SH
- Plant   – PL
- Resource investigator   – RI
- Monitor evaluator   – ME
- Team worker   – TM
- Completer finisher   – CF

The company worker/implementor

ROLE:

- Translates general ideas and plans into practical working objectives.
- Gets down to action.
- Breaks things into tasks and actions.
- Delivers actions and results.

METHODS:

- Helps ensure the team's objectives have been properly established and that any tasks have been clearly defined...
- Clarifies any practical details and deals with them.

- Maintains a steady, systematic approach.

- Is calm under pressure and reliable.

- Perseveres in the face of difficult and challenging targets.

- Provides practical support to other team members.

BEHAVIOURS TO AVOID:

- Un-constructive criticism of other team members' ideas and suggestions.

- Lack of flexibility. Company worker's have a high efficiency concern.

- Being resistant to new ideas or innovations.

As a manager, a Company worker or Implementor's strengths are their ability to define objectives and practical details. They are also very effective in introducing and maintaining procedures and structures. In organizations they are often promoted because of their inherent organizing abilities and skills.

The co-ordinator/chair

ROLE:

- Controls and organizes the activities of the team, making best use of the resources available.

- Pulls the team together.

- Stands back and helicopters above the team.

- Able to get people working together.

METHODS:

- Encourages the team members to achieve the team's objectives by helping them identify their roles and contributions.

- Encourages people to put the team objectives before their own.

- Provides positive feedback on individual performance.

- Smoothes over disagreements and inter-team competition with keen people insight and understanding. Uses tact and diplomacy to control and manage.

- Identifies weaknesses in the team's composition and organizes and develops the team to neutralise any weaknesses.

- Co-ordinates resources.

- Exercises self-discipline and perseverance. Acts as a focal point for the team's effort, especially when under pressure.

- Delegates effectively.

BEHAVIOURS TO AVOID:

- Not recognising enough the abilities of the team. Not using all of the team resources.

- Competing with other team types.

- Failing to add a creative, innovative or challenging aspect to their role.

- Abdicating the leadership role in the face of strong competition (particularly from Shapers and possibly Plants).

As a manager, a Chair or Co-ordinator is in a good position to lead the team. They are comfortable standing back from the detail and can mobilise people to tackle the issues. Their effective inter-personal skills also mean that people will listen and take their lead from an effective Chair.

The shaper

ROLE:

- Makes things happen.

- Gives shape and strong direction to the activities of the team.

- Injects energy and drive into a team's proceedings.

METHODS:

- Directs the team's focus setting objectives and clear priorities.

- Adopts a wide perspective of the team's goals and helps individuals understand their roles and contributions.

- Exerts a strong directive influence on the team's discussions. Summarises outcomes in terms of objectives and targets.

- Will often appear impatient and in a rush.

- Focuses on progress and achievements. Intervenes when the team wanders from their objectives.

- Challenges others when they purse other directions.

- Can be argumentative and dismissive of people who do not move as fast as themselves.

BEHAVIOURS TO AVOID:

- An overly directive style that assumes undue authority.

- Being too directive when making summaries, appraisals or interventions.

- Not being tactful. Overly blunt or even rude and insensitive to the needs of others.

- Becoming isolated or remote from the team. Losing identity as a team member.

- Being seen as too egotistic.

- Competing with other team members, particularly the Plant and the Monitor Evaluator.

A Shaper performs best when operating in a team of peers. If they find themselves in a formal leadership position they may well need to adopt more Co-ordinator type behaviours. This may require more involvement in routine activities and more self-discipline. Shapers normally focus on a broadbrush approach to getting things done. They have little time for the detail and want to drive forward. They also need to watch that their insensitivity to the needs of others does not in the long-term create problems for them. Tact and diplomacy is not always a high priority for shapers.

The plant

ROLE:

- Acts as a primary source of ideas and innovation for the team.

- Creative – an agent provocateur.

- An independent perspective.

METHODS:

- Concentrates their attention on the big issues and major strategies.

- Formulates new and often radical ideas and approaches

- Looks for possible breakthroughs in approaches and methods.

- Times their contributions; presenting proposals at appropriate and inappropriate moments.

BEHAVIOURS TO AVOID:

- Attempting to demonstrate their capabilities over too wide a field.

- Contributing ideas for reasons of self interest and indulgence rather than the team's needs and so alienating the team.

- Taking offence when their ideas are evaluated, criticised and rejected. Sulking and refusing to make any further contributions to the team.

- Becoming too inhibited about putting ideas forward, especially in dominant, extrovert, or over-critical groups. Being intimidated or alternatively arguing with Shapers.

A Plant needs to exercise self-discipline and be prepared to listen to team members' comments on their ideas and proposals (particularly their Monitor Evaluator colleague(s)). If found in a leadership role a Plant must not let the stresses of controlling the team stifle their creative input.

In non-directive roles a Plant should expect to be used as a strong team resource; devoting their energies and talents towards establishing their role as a creative thinker and ideas person.

The resource investigator

- Explores the team's outside resources and develops useful contacts for the team.

- Harnesses resources for the team.

- A networker and free agent.

METHODS:

- Makes excellent contacts quickly. Develops effective and useful relationships and allies for the team.

- Uses their interest in new ideas and approaches to explore outside possibilities. Introduces new people and resources to the team.

- Develops their role as the team's main point of contact with outside groups. Keeps up-to-date with new and related developments that may be helpful to the team's work.

- Helps maintain good relationships in the team and encourages team members to make best use of their talents, especially when the team is under pressure.

BEHAVIOURS TO AVOID:

- Becoming too involved with their own ideas at the expense of exploring others.

- Rejecting ideas or information before submitting them to the team.

- Relaxing too much when the pressure is off.

- Getting involved in wasteful or unproductive activities. This often results from the RI's natural sociability.

Resource Investigators are skilled communicators with a creative outlook. They are vital to helping bring new resources into a team and their networking capabilities make them invaluable.

The Monitor Evaluator

ROLE:

- Analyses ideas and suggestions.

- Evaluates ideas and approaches for their feasibility and practical value.

- Deals with facts.

- Introduces a high level of critical thinking ability to any team.

METHODS:

- Uses high levels of critical thinking ability to assess issues and plans.

- Balances an experimenting outlook with a critical assessment.

- Builds on others' suggestions or ideas. Helps the team to turn ideas into practical applications.

- Makes firm but practical and realistic arguments against the adoption of unsound approaches to problems.

- Is diplomatic when challenging suggestions.

BEHAVIOURS TO AVOID

- Using their critical thinking ability at the team's expense.

- Tactless and destructive criticism of colleagues' suggestions. Liable to upset others because of this.

- Negative thinking; allowing critical thinking skills to outweigh their openness to new ideas. Provoking a 'You always see reasons why it cannot be done!' type of response.

- Competitive behaviour with others.

- Lowering the team's morale by being excessively critical and objective.

- Ignoring other peoples' passion or emotional commitment to an idea.

A successful Monitor Evaluator combines high critical thinking skills with a practical outlook. When a Monitor Evaluator is a team leader they need to ensure that they do not dominate other members of the team and stifle contributions. When in a non-directive role a Monitor Evaluator has the challenge of making their voice heard and not appearing threatening to colleagues. If they can avoid a tendency towards undue scepticism and cynicism their strengths will help them develop their management capability.

The team worker

ROLE:

- Strong team player and member.

- Helps individual team members to contribute.

- Promotes and maintains team spirit and effectiveness.

METHODS:

- Applies themselves to the task.

- Observes the strengths and weaknesses of team members.

- Supports team members in developing their strengths, e.g. builds on suggestions and contributions.

- Helps individuals manage their weaknesses by personal advice and assistance.

- Selfless in outlook.

- Improves the team communications and builds their relationships.

- Fosters a strong sense of team spirit by setting an example.

BEHAVIOURS TO AVOID:
- Competing for status or control in the team.

- Aligning with one team member against another.

- Avoiding dealing with conflict situations.

- Delaying tough decisions.

The team worker role can be exercised at different levels within a team. As a team leader manager any Team Worker should see their role as a delegator and developer of people. The team worker's qualities of conscientiousness and perseverance will help ensure that projects are completed to time and to the necessary levels of cost and quality.

The completer finisher

ROLE:
- Ensures all the team's efforts are as near perfect as possible.

- Ensures that tasks are completed and that nothing is overlooked.

- Injects urgency into problems.

- Attention to detail.

METHODS:

- Perfectionist – looks for errors or omissions; especially those that may result from unclear responsibilities.

- Works on tasks where attention to detail and precision are important.

- Looks for mistakes in detail.

- Actively identifies work or tasks that require more detailed attention.

- Raises the standards of all the team's activities.

- Maintains a sense of urgency and priority.

BEHAVIOURS TO AVOID:

- Unnecessary emphasis on detail at the expense of the overall plan and direction.

- Negative thinking or destructive criticism.

- Lowering team morale by excessive worrying.

- Appearing slow moving or lacking in enthusiasm.

A Completer Finisher role can be exercised at different levels within a team and can be easily combined with another role. As a manager a Completer Finisher needs to pay careful attention to their delegation skills and to keep unnecessary interference with team members to a minimum. In a junior role a Completer Finisher will need to develop tact and discretion so as to avoid earning a reputation as a 'nit picker and worrier.' CF's also tend to possess a nervous drive that needs to be controlled and directed if it is to have positive results.

Figure 6 shows how some of the roles might stereo-typically work in a project team.

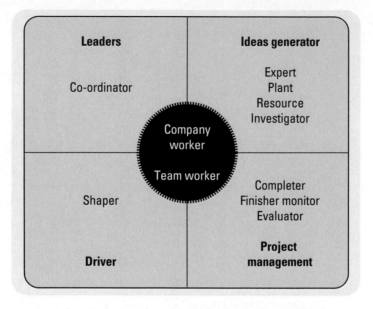

FIGURE 6: PROJECT TEAM WORKING ROLES

So you can see that from a relatively simple questionnaire you can generate a powerful analysis of preferences that people have when operating in teams. On client projects that are likely to involve some degree of team working and real complexity the early use of Belbin's approach can really start a team off in the right way. It also of course, helps us as internal consultants assess our own strengths and weaknesses in terms of team leading. We can then develop a strategy with the team to deal with any development gaps.

The attraction of Belbin's approach is that it clearly shows how important it is to have a range of skills and capabilities in order to deliver a strong project team. But at the same time you also need to consider the type of consultancy project you might be undertaking and what that might mean in terms of the types of Belbin preferences you require. If you are trying to break new ground and develop some highly innovative approaches you might need a lot of Plant or

Resource Investigator preferences. Equally if you are building a complex new production line you may require lots of Implementor and Monitor Evaluator type preferences.

Figure 7 provides some questions that you can reflect on with regard to this issue.

What consultancy task or project do you need to complete?
– Innovative breakthrough solutions?
– Detailed operational implementation tasks?

What is the balance of your proposed project team?

Do you have the right balance?

Do you need to consider reviewing the team's make-up for the project?

What are your preferences as the project leader?

FIGURE 7: BELBIN'S TEAM TYPES – MY PROJECT TEAM

In some cases as an internal consultant you will be asked to take on the overall management of the implementation process perhaps being supported by an expert project manager. In other assignments you may be asked to provide assistance on a less involved basis. In either situation, your involvement during the implementation stage is important because very often only you and your client will have an overall understanding of the project's background and aims.

CHAPTER **THREE**

Marketing internal consultancy

Marketing internal consultancy

Getting in and contracting with your client

The first stage in our consulting cycle involves getting in front of clients in order to discuss the possibility of providing some kind of assistance. In moving from a classic support function to an internal consultancy perspective, you will need to plan how you are going to market your services. For many people new to the consultancy role this is a major departure from past practices. Having to actively promote your services as opposed to having a ready stream of internal customers comes as a major challenge. How you promote your services will of course depend on the objectives or operating guidelines your organization has provided. In some cases you may market your services on a very small scale; having been guaranteed a regular amount of work from existing clients. In other situations you may find yourself in constant competition with external consultants to win internal projects.

Like any form of strategy the first step to developing a marketing strategy involves answering some very critical and fundamental questions. This demands that you step back from any the day-to-day operational pressures and commitments and look at future goals and objectives. If you are working as a consulting unit or team, then you will need to address these issues with your colleagues. Whilst these questions seem very straightforward, experience shows that they generate significant discussion and debate. So to complete this planning phase consider spending quality time on the activity, perhaps a full or half day debating your responses.

- What type of consulting business are we in?

- Who are our clients?

- What are their needs?

- What are the results and benefits of our services?

- What are our qualities?

- What are our objectives as a consulting unit?

- What potential barriers or obstacles exist for us?

- Who are our competitors?

- What risks are involved?

- What overall strategy should we adopt to become successful?

For illustrative purposes we have included some example answers to these questions. They cover possible responses from groups such as training and development through to information technology departments. Like all strategy development there are no simple answers to these questions. You and your colleagues have to do the hard thinking, as only you can develop the relevant responses for your operation.

Developing your marketing strategy

What sort of consulting group are we?

We are a small highly focused consulting team providing value added services in the areas of software systems design and support. We specialise in the development of world class web-based applications to enhance organizational efficiency and business performance.

Who are our clients?

Our clients are the senior executive and middle management groups across the organization.

What do our clients require from us?

Our clients require a highly flexible and responsive service in the areas of web-based applications and technology. They demand a high level of technical support and ongoing consultancy that compares with the best that is available externally.

What services and products do we provide?

We provide a range of business focused training and development solutions as well as a portfolio of skills development programmes, self development and learning resources – that include web-based solutions, CDs and manuals.

We provide clients with the skills to help them maximise their investment in information technology with a key focus on mission critical business processes.

What is our clients' perception of us?

Our client image is that of a high quality business focused and customer responsive unit that delivers real value added solutions on limited resources.

How do our clients regard our value to them?

Our clients' perceptions of 'our prices' and value is that we are highly cost effective and competitive in relation to other providers and that we provide high value added services

How do we intend to develop our client base?

We will seek more opportunities through our existing client base. We do not propose to develop new streams of client activity at this particular stage of our development

How will we operate and distribute our services?

We plan to provide and deliver our services by allocating a dedicated individual to each business unit. This will ensure that every client manager has a direct contact to our services capability. Our clients will work on a daily basis with someone who shares a detailed understanding of their business challenges and operating environment.

How will we communicate and promote our services?

We will promote our services through our existing client base and by actively promoting our successes through the organization's various web sites, seminars, newsletters and promotional literature. We also run regular briefings to update our clients on our latest service offerings.

Financial/budgetary objectives

We will achieve the following objectives in line with our agreed operating guidelines which are to recover our total operating costs from our internal and, wherever possible, external consulting activities.

Answering these questions demands a high degree of self-analysis and criticism. It is no use thinking that everything you do is excellent if your clients have a different perspective. You might be working twelve hour days and think you are doing a great job but it could be that your client is not aware of what you are doing. So you must question all existing activities. You have to be clear as to your starting base and evaluate your past track record.

All strategy involves developing a clear focus and that demands that you make choices and decide between different options. By spending quality time debating these choices you are more likely to develop a clear focus for your future activities.

Conducting a client demand analysis

Another key planning activity that you can conduct in parallel to the one above, involves a client demand analysis. Indeed, this activity can really assist the development of your marketing strategy. The objective of this exercise is to identify who your current clients are and what it is that they want from you in terms of services or products. Figure 8 shows an example form that you can use. Again the process is relatively simple in design but very powerful in terms of impact.

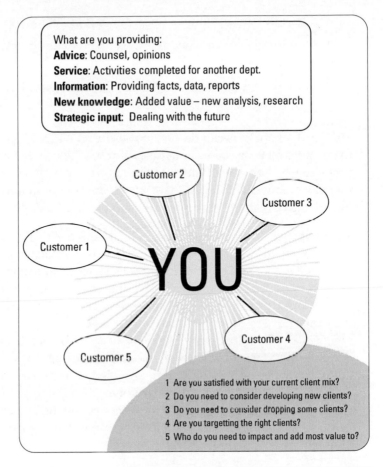

What are you providing:
Advice: Counsel, opinions
Service: Activities completed for another dept.
Information: Providing facts, data, reports
New knowledge: Added value – new analysis, research
Strategic input: Dealing with the future

Customer 2
Customer 3
Customer 1
YOU
Customer 4
Customer 5

1 Are you satisfied with your current client mix?
2 Do you need to consider developing new clients?
3 Do you need to consider dropping some clients?
4 Are you targetting the right clients?
5 Who do you need to impact and add most value to?

FIGURE 8: MAPPING YOUR CUSTOMERS / CLIENTS

To complete this analysis you are required to think of every possible client group that you serve. You then need to identify what service you currently provide them with. In most support functions the services provided revolve around five key areas:

1   Giving advice.

2   Offering some kind of service – a physical transaction.

3   Providing information – facts, data, reports.

4   Providing new knowledge – adding something new to the organization.

5   Strategic contribution – adding something strategic to the organization.

This form of analysis can be very powerful as it forces you to consider all your clients and the extent to which you currently satisfy their needs. You may typically discover that you focus on some clients more than others and that you may have some very influential clients for whom you do very little.

The next step is to reflect on your analysis and decide if you are happy with your current level of client and service mix? After reflection, you may find yourself deciding to reduce your services to certain clients and increasing the effort with others in order to develop a stronger relationships. Such decisions have to be set against your broader strategy and what you decide will deliver long-term success. You may also conclude that you are not focusing enough on the higher value added activities of providing new knowledge or making a strategic contribution. This might involve you adjusting the types of activity you get involved in. Of course giving advice can be a highly significant contribution but it does depend on what areas you are working in.

As with all strategic planning type processes there are no right or wrong answers to these questions. You will obtain maximum benefit by working through these two processes with your colleagues. Ultimately you will need to make clear decisions about your objectives, role and operating style. You want to emerge from any analysis with a clear focus and sense of direction that will assist you as you develop your medium to long-term contribution.

What clients look for

To develop even more detailed responses to the above questions you need to constantly put yourself in the clients' shoes and ask yourself 'Why should I buy from these people?' This is an immensely powerful question to ask as a consultant. You have to think about your client's needs and focus on what the client is looking for when selecting consultants.

> Before you present your proposals to your clients, remember to put yourself in their shoes and apply the 'so what' challenge. If you can't come up with a satisfactory answer don't expect your clients to buy in. Talk the language of the business when framing and presenting your proposals. Anticipate the questions you will be asked; these are likely to contain the objections to your proposals. Work through these and you are close to achieving buy in.
>
> *Tracey Norbury, Development Adviser, HSBC*

Tangibles

Clients look for tangibles such as business performance and efficiency improvements, reduced costs, improved revenues, enhanced levels of customer service. These are probably the most important factors that will get your clients interested in your services. Harness your marketing efforts around these types of hard business benefits.

Business understanding

Clients buy from people they feel understand their business challenges, problems and issues. Ask yourself how well you understand your clients' businesses? How much time do you spend really trying to find out what the current pressures are that they face? If the answer is not much, then start developing your knowledge base by finding out as much as you can about their challenges.

Methodologies

Clients are impressed by proven methodologies that detail precise ways of implementing change. They indicate that the consultant has a well thought out approach that can be visibly seen. Methodologies provide clients with a high degree of comfort that the consultant knows what they are doing and is professional in their approach. Methodologies dominate the areas of production and information technology but they can also be adopted in other consulting areas such as training and development and change management . So be alert to the possibilities of using or adapting such methodologies and techniques to your field of consulting work.

Reassurance

Remember that any client commissioning a consultancy service is putting himself or herself in a position of risk. They are in effect placing their confidence and trust in someone to deliver something that is of great important to them. Any client therefore, needs a strong degree of reassurance in a consultant's competence and track record.

Many clients after hiring a consultant will be asking themselves whether they have made the right decision. Clients like to have confidence and peace of mind with regard to their decisions. So be sure to deal with these less tangible aspects of the client relationship by keeping very close to your client, communicating and advising them of progress and offering constant reassurance. Staying close to your clients and being proactive in the relationship is central to developing a strong client sense of confidence.

Consulting team operating statement

- 'Use the Nestec Productivity Team (NPT) as a career development step
- 3C's Commitment, Credibility, Confidence
- Find Synergies (most wheels have been invented)
- Use the brainpower of our employees
- 'We know how but don't apply'
- Focus on the how not the what – 'it's not just what you do, it's the way you do it'
- Stop! before compromising commitment'

Operating Statement

Nestle Nestec Productivity Team, Vevey, Switzerland
Courtesy of Curt Blattner

But if that is what clients look for, what is it that they are actually buying from a consultant? Well, there are two critical things that clients buy from any internal consultant

Identifying the real client need

Part of your role as a consultant will be to help your client translate their broad concerns and issues into specific needs that can then be satisfied through your intervention and support. A large part of consultancy work involves challenging your client's thoughts so as to uncover their real needs – what it really is that they want addressed. Very often clients are not clear as to what they want. That is why time must be devoted in probing and trying to identify the real problem areas for your client. What a client initially says they want may not be what they need. Your initial contact and involvement with a client involves trying to resolve and define their real underlying business needs.

Solutions

Ultimately a client wants a solution to their problem. Products or methodologies that assist you in achieving this goal are highly valuable but never lose sight of the fact that it is the final solution that matters most to your client. Therefore when developing your marketing strategy and plans focus on how your involvement and solutions can help your client solve their problems.

Helpful tips

Never ever confuse what you are trying to sell with what your client wants to buy.

You must always address your client's real needs and not what you think they need. It is one of the greatest faults of consultants to focus on their solution at the expense of the client's problem. Be sure that you constantly address the problem as defined by the client and not the elegance of your methodology or process.

Following this golden rule will ensure you stay client focused.

Beginning to market yourself – recognising your starting point

Once you get out into the real world of clients you will secure different reactions to your approaches. Figure 9 below illustrates the range of potential client reactions that might greet any marketing activity you conduct. Clearly it makes sense to focus efforts on those clients who either express a genuine interest in your services or actively seek your assistance. In the longer term you also need to remain in touch with potential clients who are aware of your services but who may not have requested any help. You cannot afford to ignore these clients as they may represent a valuable source of future work for you. Indeed you may well need to spend time trying to understand why they have not contacted you. But be wary of expending lots of energy and effort on people who have no intention of ever wanting to use your services. Life is too hard to waste effort on people who are never going to buy your services. Better to focus your efforts on people who understand what you have to offer and are prepared to work in a co-operative way. These are the sorts of clients you want to cultivate.

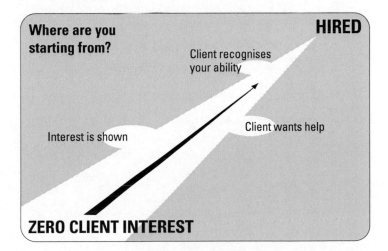

FIGURE 9: MARKETING INTERNAL CONSULTANCY

Marketing to senior management

Who are your key clients?

When trying to focus your marketing activities reflect on the classic Pareto Principle of 80-20. It is another simple but powerful way to focus on your marketing efforts. In marketing the principle suggests that 20% of your clients account for 80% of your workload and success. The critical marketing question to be addressed is whether you know which 20% of your client base is actually delivering your success? Referring to your earlier client analysis may help you come up with the right answer.

So constantly review, question and analyse your marketing approach to test it's effectiveness. In most organizations a very important element of the 20% is likely to be the senior management cadre. They of course, have the power to hire you and to action new projects and initiatives. So really challenge yourself on how much work you do with the key leaders in your organization. By concentrating marketing efforts on senior management you frequently gain the following benefits:

- Bigger and higher value added projects.

- Referrals to other parts of the organization.

- Access to strong sources of influence.

- Strong resource allocation.

- A power-base to appeal to when times are difficult.

Helpful tip

Put yourself in your client's shoes and remember that all clients want to:

- Be listened to
- Feel important and respected
- Have their needs addressed
- Know in simple clear terms how you can help them

How to sell to senior management

When selling to senior management there are three key steps to follow:

1 Understand your client's motivations

In any consultancy selection process you need to identify at an early stage who the key decision-makers on the client side are. Once you have identified them (often there will be more than one) you should try to identify their individual needs and wants. In doing so remember that managers are not all motivated by the same thing. For some it is not always about solving the problem. So examine the range of personal needs that might exist around the table. Reflect on some of the classic needs:

- Solving the problem.
- Exploiting new opportunities that will arise as a result of the project.
- Securing personal credit – 'It will make me look good'.

- To criticise a previous decision or approach – 'It's pay-back time!'

- Political ambitions within the organization – 'I need this to show them...'.

> Real change can only happen when you have an enthusiastic business sponsor who is personally committed. They can open doors and engage other decision-makers. In return, the sponsor looks to you as the internal consultant, to understand the business and provide them with workable solutions. An effective working relationship is built on trust and a clear agreement as to what is to be delivered.
>
> *Tracey Norbury, Development Adviser, HSBC*

Never overlook the desire for personal gain or political ambition. Many senior managers are always looking for projects that can make them look good in their organization. It is the nature of large organizations that power games are frequently played. So be alert to hidden agendas and personal ambitions.

By focusing on this other aspect of the 'selling' process and trying to identify different types of client need, greatly enhances your chances of success in connecting with clients when pitching for a project.

Define the business priorities

By skillfully defining and articulating a client's key business priorities you can easily identify the outputs or deliverables that the client is seeking to achieve. Always reflect these priorities in your terms of reference so that your client instantly recognises them. Better still try to add some new insights for your client around their business priorities. This really impresses clients and gives them confidence in your overall approach and involvement.

State the benefits of your involvement

When selling a product or service professional marketing people always distinguish clearly between features and benefits. Features are merely aspects of your approach such as 'we use the latest technology!' or 'we have a detailed methodology.' Features are interesting, but what your client really wants to hear is what the technology will do to solve the problem. Benefits are what normally result from features and it is benefits that clients really like. For example a benefit of using a particular type of technology is that it will produce a faster and quicker solution. That is likely to be of far more interest to your client as it involves saving time or money.

So, whilst methodologies and techniques are an important and part of your marketing approach, focusing on the benefits is where you should really focus your arguments and efforts. To major on the features of your involvement is a classic mistake that people make when selling consultancy. So always ensure that you stay results-focused and highlight the benefits of any approach or solution you offer. Ask yourself what will your approach or solution do to improve the business in very hard and tangible terms? Think bottom-line results!

Some practical tips to improve your marketing effort

- Solve the problems of the Chief Executive Officer and Board.

- Focus on your organization's pressure points – find out where the business is hurting and see if you can help. It always pays as a consultant to be business and performance focused.

- Use factual bottom-line business performance measures to promote your activities – demonstrate a real value added contribution.

- Work with those managers who are converted to your approach and services. Don't waste valuable time and effort on managers who will never understand or appreciate your work. Focus on people who value your input.

- Cultivate word-of-mouth referrals. The best form of marketing (as well as the cheapest) is recommendations from happy and satisfied clients. So cultivate your clients to promote your work around the organization.

- Think about developing a distinct identity in your organization. Discuss the possibility of promoting a logo or newsletter which informs the organization about your role and services.

- Network and seize all opportunities to present your work to others. If asked to make a presentation at the annual sales conference, do it! See it as an opportunity to talk about a successful project. Better still do the presentation in partnership with your client.

- Audit your staff to check that they are displaying client focused behaviours. All your efforts can be wasted if the person answering your phone is less than professional in their attitude towards existing and potential clients.

- Develop your own personal network of contacts both internally and externally to your organization. Take people out to lunch and talk about your projects.

- Invite externally speakers into your organization and invite influential managers along. It helps to position yourself as someone who is trying to add value to the organization.

- Visit other companies and organizations. Find out about best practice in your field of operation. Your ability to comment on such matters gives you credibility, power and influence.

- Collaborate with other internal consultants from other organizations. They can help improve your skill base and give you new ideas.

- Send relevant articles of your work or of general business to key clients. It is an easy, low cost way of keeping yourself in front of them. If the article is relevant they may well mention it next time you meet; alternatively you have something that you can casually raise as a discussion topic with them. You may even find that your client asks you to follow up on some of the points contained in the article.

- Keep a clear record of all your client meetings. Don't lose touch with your clients. Clients do not like consultants who ring up because they have run out of work as it gives them a negative perception of how you value them and view them. Effective consultants work hard at maintaining relationships even when no work is on offer. Always be thinking about the longer term and remember all client contact is a form of marketing.

- Remember that most business comes from your existing client base. So try to actively promote your work and keep your clients in touch with other types of work you are engaged in.

- Finally, stay alert to all opportunities. Any project, no matter how small has the potential to develop into other areas and larger assignments.

Internal consultancy case study   autodesk®

Background

Matthias Behrens is the Director for Business Process Management at Autodesk. Founded in 1982, Autodesk, Inc., is the world's leading design software and digital content company. It offers solutions for professionals in building design, geographic information systems, manufacturing, digital media and wireless data services. It has more than 3,600 employees located in offices around the world. With about four million customers in over 150 countries, it is one of the largest PC software companies in the world.

Matthias and his team are providing services around project and business process management globally to the Autodesk organization.

Internal Consultancy at Autodesk

My team has a very broad role. The main goal of our work is to help the organization to improve its ability in executing critical change efforts. To do this we provide a variety of tools, methods and services around project and process management. Whilst most of these services are an optional offering to the organization, we also have an additional responsibility to ensure that project teams adhere to various standards. This dual role requires us to perform a careful and difficult balancing act.

We have a wide variety of customers for our services. It begins with Senior Management who not only want investments to go to the most valuable projects but who also want to see them effectively implemented. Project sponsors in turn want to see their proposed initiatives approved and funded. Finally, project managers and their teams want help with applying project and process management tools and techniques.

All of our clients are eager to ensure that any project and process management input we provide is not adding an administrative burden to their work. It is a constant challenge for us to get the right balance: enforcing certain global standards without losing credibility as a real partner in trying to provide valuable consulting services. So to be effective in our role we have developed a set of working practices, behaviours and attitudes that help us to address some of the challenges we face.

Most of our work involves 'change' and helping people go about their work in a different way. However, many of the solutions we provide are not automatically perceived as valuable. Autodesk is an organization that values speed, flexibility and risk-taking among its core values.

People naturally worry our suggestions might slow them down or increase their work burden. So we often meet some initial resistance when we try to help. To be successful we first try to understand our colleagues' motivations, needs and worries.

All project sponsors and business managers have different needs and some of these invariably conflict. It is imperative to understand what these needs are and to develop individual strategies to serve these requirements. The internal consultant's role is not about selling standard solutions but trying to solve the client's individual problem. This requires a very different belief; that of **seeing our customers not as colleagues but as clients**! Clients who can choose to take our services and advice or go elsewhere. Such clients have to be persuaded that we provide real value.

A second belief that we have had to abandon is that it is not just **expertise that is critical to our success**. As experts in project and process management it is very easy to fall into a lecturing mode: telling the client how to run their project, highlighting mistakes and generally being prescriptive. This approach inevitably results in resistance. To be successful we have learnt that we have to listen to the client's problems and try to really understand the underlying drivers. More often we help by asking questions rather than by giving advice. We frequently facilitate the process for project teams to find answers to their problems. **Involving the client** in finding the solution – rather than presenting it to them – seems to be a successful approach for us.

Being experts in project and process management, we naturally use a **standardised approach to our consulting process** and treat most of our engagements as a formal project.

Whilst some managers can see it initially as some kind of overhead, we develop and produce a formal project engagement charter at the start of each project. We then follow a simple and clearly phased process to run the projects. In the following pages you will see how we approach this contracting phase with an example of our project charter or terms of reference documentation. This is a key document and a major element of our client management approach.

For us the charter documentation has the following advantages:

- It ensures expectations are properly set for all the parties involved at the outset of the project.

- Key factors like timelines, boundaries, stakeholders and deliverables are clearly defined and discussed.

- The client as well as the consultant has clear visibility on where we should be during the life-cycle of the project.

As we develop our approach many challenges remain for us:

Establishing real measures of success are a constant challenge. As consultants we provide a lot of advice and manage without authority. As such our share of any project success is extremely difficult to measure. By definition the job is more about influencing and persuading than having control. Wrongly set measures can have the detrimental effect of pushing consultants into an expert mode, trying to push clients to perform certain activities so that the consultants' goals are achieved.

As an internal consultant you have to work out how you can fit into the normal performance management process within the organization. Goals need to be very carefully formulated and often less SMART objectives might be desirable, which is of course, contrary to conventional performance management thinking.

As our services are 'free-of-charge' a standard success measure that applies to external consultants – the generation of consulting fees – is also not applicable.

Dealing with remoteness is another key issue for the team. We are working in a globally distributed organization. Personal contact with our internal customers is often limited to phone conversations. Sometimes it might be months before we are able to meet some of our clients face-to-face. Working across many different time zones means we have to communicate via email or at unearthly hours and inconvenient locations. While frequent travel, use of video and phone equipment or online web tools can ease this problem, they do not remove it.

At the same time the internal consultant's role requires a high level of influencing skills. The ability to read a client's body language and facial expressions or to have informal water cooler conversations is a significant skill requirement. Outstanding interpersonal skills have to be combined with the necessary technical skills to achieve maximum impact.

Operating as an internal consultant continues to pose a unique set of challenges. It certainly requires a change in attitude and approach to the normal support specialist role. But once you master the skills and techniques the rewards are immense. The prize is an ability to influence the organization at all levels, positive client feedback and in turn a constant demand for your services. For anyone embarking on the journey – I would say enjoy it for it is a great way to grow and develop your skills!

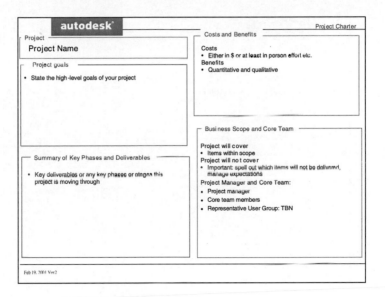

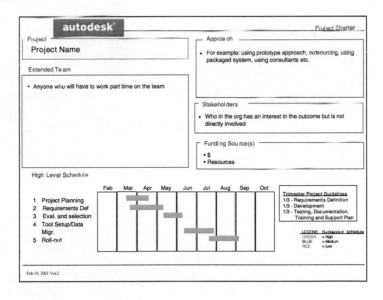

Template 1

autodesk®

Project

Project Name

Assumptions/Constraints

- For example assumptions of availability of resources, technical tools etc.

Dependencies

- Any other projects or decisions that the project depends upon

Issues / Risks

- What can make the project fail?

Flexibility Matrix

	Least Flexible	Less Flexible	More Flexible	Most Flexible
Qualit			X	
Resources		X		
Scope	X			
Time				X

Note: Each flexibility option can be checked only once.

Feb 19, 2001 Ver.2

Template 2

autodesk®

Project Charter

Project

Project Name

Post Project Ownership

- Who owns after go-live date, are the organizations aware?

Success Criteria

- How would the sponsors and stakeholders evaluate if the project was successful?

Alternatives / Supplemental

- if we did not take the outlined approach to the project, which alternatives were considered (and why not chosen?)
- if we did not do the project at all, do we have alternatives?
- any other comment?

Approvals

Sponsor Name 1

Sponsor Name 2

Sponsor Name 3

Sponsor Name 4

Feb 19, 2001 Ver.2

CHAPTER **FOUR**

Managing initial client meetings

FOUR
Managing initial client meetings

Initial client meetings are the starting point from which you begin building a client base in your organization. In most cases you will have been invited by a potential or existing client to discuss a problem and explore the possibility of providing some assistance. Your ability to handle and manage initial client meetings professionally is vital to your success. Initial meetings are the first step in promoting your involvement and expertise to clients. Having the capability to enter a potential client's office and subsequently emerge having sold your services is a demanding and challenging role.

It may well be the case that at an initial meeting you already know your potential client. However, be wary of making assumptions about how to deal with your clients. It is very easy to think that someone you have worked with for many years is simply an old colleague. You may feel that you can simply turn up for the meeting and have a good old chat with them. This is not the approach to take. You need to view former colleagues with a very different 'client' perspective.

Initial meetings have to be conducted with a high degree of professionalism. Simply arriving at someone's office with the intention of having a friendly discussion is not the way to impress clients. Throughout the meeting you want to send strong messages to your potential client that you value and appreciate their time. You have to show that you are keen to assist the client in any problems or challenges they maybe facing.

The objectives of initial client meetings are to:

- Learn about your client's operation.

- Understand your client's problems or challenges.

- Determine whether you might be able to help them.

- Assess if you can provide assistance in the necessary timescales.

- Assess if you are interested in the problem.

- Begin building a client relationship.

- Reflect on the client's problem.

- Agree the next steps or withdraw from any further involvement.

The essential rules for managing initial client meetings

The most important rule in any initial meeting is to get your client talking. Getting through an initial meeting in a thorough and professional manner requires you to follow a set of clear guidelines. If you adhere to them you will find that your initial meetings run successfully. So ensure that you:

- Always arrive on time – never be late even if your client is (remember that is their privilege).

- Introduce your colleagues (if two consultants are interviewing).

- Carry out clear and focused introductions – who you are, where you are from, the nature of your skills.

- Outline your understanding of the broad purpose and objectives of the meeting.

- Check the amount of time your client has available for the meeting.

Helpful tips

- A powerful question to ask your client at all initial meetings is 'What would success look like if this project were to be successful and work?'

- This question can also be followed by, 'And what would people be doing differently as a result of the proposed initiative – what would they be doing that they are not doing now?'

- In most instances these questions will secure powerful responses from your client. They will define in their own terms exactly what they want the project or your involvement to deliver. You will be surprised how quickly you obtain your clients fundamental requirements.

- Obtain your client's agreement to the meeting's objectives and timescales – this forms the basis of a contract for your meeting. You want to find out as much as you can about the client's situation.

- Discuss and clarify your understanding of the background and issues by asking lots of open-ended questions.

- Summarise and reflect back your client's comments regularly to ensure you have understood what has been said.

- Ask for access to any supporting or relevant materials concerning the problem – reports, documents that might be supplied during or after your meeting.

- Check for any areas that your client does not want you to get involved in. Establish the boundaries to your work.

- Agree on the results your client would like to achieve

- Be prepared to explore tentative ways to possibly solve your client's problem. Remember that it is very early to start being prescriptive about solutions.

- Summarise and agree the next steps concerning your involvement – key actions and responsibilities before your next meeting. In most cases this will mean you presenting an initial terms of reference for discussion.

- Agree a date, time and place for your next meeting.

- Agree a basis of maintaining regular contact and access to your client. For example:
  - Weekly 30 minute meeting to review progress.
  - One page summary of key actions to be sent to your client every week.
  - Monthly review meeting with your client and the project team.

- Agree a form of communication with your client to announce your involvement on the project. Agree a distribution list of interested parties. Offer to draft this letter for your client to review and then circulate.

- Keep a record of your meeting.

- Write to your client confirming what was discussed and any agreed action points. Also confirm the date, time and place of your next meeting.

Things to avoid at initial meetings

Appearing unprepared or unprofessional is probably the worst impression to give any client at an initial meeting. Below is a list containing some classic errors. Avoid them at all costs.

- Not stating your objectives for the meeting.

- Not listening to the client.

- Talking too much at your client.

- Displaying arrogant or aggressive behaviour.

- Being inflexible in your interview approach.

- Running out of time to deal with all the issues.

- Being drawn into making personal comments about other people or departments in your organization.

- Voicing recommendations too early – remember it may not be a systems or people issue!

- Demonstrating a lack of confidence or credibility.

- Leaving the meeting with the wrong problem.

- Not being proactive enough in suggesting how events should progress to the next stage.

How to convey respect, openness and understanding at an initial client meeting

Respect

- Arrive on time.

- Be polite and courteous.

- Acknowledge your client's opinions and respect their values.

- Agree a contract for your meeting – objectives, timing etc.

- Allow your client time to talk about their concerns.

- Give your client full attention.

- Avoid patronising comments or observations.

- Avoid being judgemental – just listen.

Openness

- Be clear and open about your objectives.

- At this early stage avoid matters that may involve organizational politics or intrigue.

- Be prepared to admit on your part any errors, mistakes or misunderstandings.

- Share some of your thoughts and ideas with the client.

- Be honest about explaining the scope and limitations of your work.

- Be honest in your answers – if you don't know then say you don't know.

- Challenge your client if you do not understand anything. It is better to ask now rather than later. Asking later may make you look foolish.

Understanding

- Demonstrate a real appreciation of your client's position by informed questioning.

- Regularly summarise your client's answers and their comments.

- Recognise that some clients may have strong feelings on certain issues.

Initial client meetings consultant's template

As part of a professional approach always attend an initial meeting with your questions prepared well in advance. This will in itself help you to project confidence and a sense of experience. At the end of an initial meeting you need to carefully record the results of your client discussions. Consider using the template at the end of this chapter to act as a focus for your questions and to record key points. The following pages provide some simple examples to illustrate how they might be used. (See over).

INITIAL MEETING FORM

Date/Time March 7, 14:00 | **Location** Head Office, Chicago

Dept/Client Name/Present VP Finance, Jan Peters, Mark Thomas

Meeting Purpose To discuss the merger of two finance departments in the New York area following the recent acquisition of a major competitor business.

What is the client reporting structure	Description of client's operation
• Jim Davies (CFO) • Carlos Mendes (VP Finance) • Jenny Bond (Manager) Erica Hoffman (Manager)	Finance functions currently process all key financial reporting activities for both businesses.

What are your clients issues

Requirement to merge two key functions following an acquisition. Each have different cultures and work processes.

Need to rationalise the staffing levels and successfully integrate new activities and workload whilst minimising any operational disruptions or delays.

Large operations – different business systems, styles and culture along with need to effect rapid integration – 4-6 months.

Initial thoughts to solve problem

Establish project team to highlight key issues.

Develop an integration strategy.

Meet staff and understand perspectives and key concerns.

Communicate intentions and set out draft timetable.

Develop resourcing and staff release schemes in line with HR department support.

Action

• Visit sites – JP, MT
• Interview key staff – MT
• Prepare integration strategy – MT and key client staff

Next meeting date/time/place

March 25, 10:00,
Head Office Chicago

Duration of meeting 2 hours

INITIAL MEETING FORM

Date / Time 12 Sept, 8am

Location Zurich Office

Dept / Name / Present IT Dept – Gert Hunzinker, David Thirill, Rolf Behr

Meeting Purpose To discuss the migration of a major customer database from an existing stand alone system to new fully integrated state of the art network.

What is the client reporting structure

- Rolf Wigand (IT Director)
- Patricia Jovenetti (Supervisor)
- Anne Dabell James Lock Jan Laube

Description of client's operation

Speciality chemical business serving small medium sized business across Europe.

Department is link to sales, marketing and accounts

What are your clients issues

Need to effect clear migration plan

Minimise disruption

Develop plan to make the switch over critical holiday period in order to lessen impact on business and customer operations

No real experience today of handling a project of this complexity

Staff reactions

Initial thoughts to solve problem

Review existing status of project with key vendors – establish exact position

Establish transition team and develop draft plan – Involvement of key stakeholders

Meet with key stakeholders on operational impact and issues

Address customer and staffing communications

Action

- Get budget – GP
- Detailed requirements meeting – DH DT
- Visit other key business sites with RW – RB

Next meeting date/time/place

18 Sept, 8am, Zurich Office

Duration of meeting 1.5 hours

Initial terms of reference

Why prepare an initial terms of reference?

The most visible and professional way in which you demonstrate to your client that you have understood their problem and requirements is by producing a terms of reference. This document serves as the 'contract' between you and your client. It will in all probability, be referenced and updated on complex projects several times during the life of an assignment. In some extreme cases, the main project objectives may even change. Clearly such changes must be documented so that the focus for the project is not lost. It is essential that any changes made to your terms of reference are discussed in detail and agreed by your client before they are implemented. No consultant has the power to change an initial terms of reference without the express agreement of their client. Only when the client has signed off any changes to the terms of reference can a project really begin.

What should the initial terms of reference contain?

The main characteristic of a quality terms of reference is that it should be clear and concise. It needs to clearly indicate what the project's objectives are and what work the consultant is proposing to do. It also needs to highlight any constraints or assumptions that you are making and also show the key stages and milestones involved in your plan. It has also to indicate your resourcing and where appropriate costs.

The key headings to use and a description of their content include the following:

BACKGROUND

- A description of the background to the work or the project.

- Identify any past problems or other relevant issues.

- Include information gained from your initial client meeting.

- Keep this section to a maximum of two paragraphs – it should provide someone new to the project with a clear and simple overview.

OBJECTIVES

- State the outcomes and business objectives that must be achieved from the work.

- State who your client is.

BOUNDARY

Document the boundaries or scope of the work to be covered. Clearly identify:

- What will be done.

- What will not be done.

- What departments will be involved.

CONSTRAINTS

Record the constraints that you are working with including:

- Time.

- People.

- Money.

- Equipment.

- Other resources.

ASSUMPTIONS

- State the assumptions you are making. For example, access to resources, client staff and financial budgets. This will indicate to your client what further information you will need.

When your initial terms of reference are signed off, there should be no assumptions left in it, as you will have either agreed or adjusted the basis on which you will carry out the work following your client discussions. For example your client has now agreed that managers will be instructed to release staff to attend your interviews. In the real world you cannot assume that this would have happened. Many projects have failed because too many assumptions were made that proved to be just that, an assumption! So if in doubt raise it as an assumption, clarify it and then remove it.

CLIENT REPORTING

State the client reporting requirements showing:

- Who on the client side will receive your reports.

- How these reports will be presented – meetings, electronic mail or paper.

- What precise format the report will take – Microsoft Word, Powerpoint etc, A4 text document or landscaped Powerpoint slides?

- When the reports will be delivered.

PROJECT DELIVERABLES

State the project deliverables indicating:

- What the deliverables will be.
- When they will be delivered.
- Note these down as milestones.

ACTIVITY TIME CHART

- Show the major tasks involved in your project and their sequence.
- Indicate when they will be done? Show the week number and completion dates.
- How long they will take.
- Who will be completing these tasks.
- Show the milestones where key deliverables will be made, e.g. presentation, report, system specification, operating procedures, client workshops.

FINANCE (WHERE APPROPRIATE)

- Show the staff fee rate for each project stage.
- Show other necessary resourcing and material costs.
- Show the total estimated budget required.

Sample initial terms of reference

Our initial terms of reference headings have been transferred onto a form that you can use for your project. Figure 10 highlights the key elements of the TOR.

BACKGROUND Description of background of work to be done. Two paragraphs maximum.

OBJECTIVE State overall business objectives. State project sponsor.

BOUNDARY What work will be done. What work will not be done. What departments will be involved.

CONSTRAINTS Note constraints in terms of time, people, equipment and money.

ASSUMPTIONS Your customers will provide you with further information. When TOR signed off, there should be no assumptions in it.

REPORTING What are reporting requirements? Who receives them? How will they be represented? When will reports be delivered? Meetings, electronic or paper.

DELIVERABLES What are you going to deliver? When are you going to deliver?

FINANCE How much will this project cost? Include cost of people, equipment and expenses.

Client sign-off

✔ BACKGROUND
✔ OBJECTIVE
✔ BOUNDARY
✔ CONSTRAINTS
✔ ASSUMPTIONS
✔ REPORTING
✔ DELIVERABLES
✔ FINANCE

FIGURE 10: PROJECT TERMS OF REFERENCE

This form can be found in the chapter on 'The Internal Consultant's Toolkit'. Review the following example and reflect on how you might incorporate this approach in your consulting work.

Remember, at this stage you are preparing an initial terms of reference based on your understanding of the project. These details will invariably change and more information will be added as the project progresses and develops.

TERMS OF REFERENCE FORM

Client Name Boris Lang IT Director	**Date** 16 August
Consultant Name Emily Goodson	**Location** Hamburg
Project Name Internal Support Department	**Start Date** 18 September

Background

- In the last two years, the Hamburg office has increased its staff from 30 to over 120. IT support for training and computer maintenance is currently supplied by two external companies. Service levels vary considerably.

- Head office have an international drive to create internal IT support sections wherever possible throughout the company to provide greater control and quality of service to our employees.

Objective

- To investigate the service level provided by the two external companies

- To document the skills required for an IT Support function.

Boundary

- Involve the senior management at Hamburg site

- Understand and document the services required

- Interview staff of external support companies

- Interview staff at Hamburg site

- Determine level of satisfaction of employees

- Do not recommend individual employees for new post

TERMS OF REFERENCE FORM

Constraints

- Details of this assignment must not be discussed with the external IT support companies

Assumptions

- Members of external IT support companies are available for interview
- Internal staff members are available for interview
- All interviewees will be available over a one week period

Reporting

- Provide a brief progress report every Friday by 14:00
- Use the internal electronic mail system

Deliverables and Milestones

- Provide a final report at the end of the assignment in 4 weeks time
- Present the findings to the IT Director

TERMS OF REFERENCE FORM

Activity Time Chart For Project:

Activity	Who	Effort	Start	Week 1	2	3	4	5	6	7	8
1. Prepare Plan	EG	0.5		***							
	BL	0.5		**							
2. Services Needed	EG	3			****						
3. Investigate Co 1	EG	2					****				
4. Investigate Co 2	EG	2						****			
5. Interview Staff	EG	4							*****		
6. Report	EG	2								****	
7. Presentation	EG	0.5									
	BL	0.5									
Total Effort:	**x days**										

Estimated Costs

Resource Name: Emily Goodson   **Rate:** 900   **Effort:** 14   **Cost:** 12,600

Resource Name: Boris Lang   **Rate:** 1,500   **Effort:** 1   **Cost:** 1,500

Resource Name: **Rate:**   **Effort:**   **Cost:**

Resource Name: **Rate:**   **Effort:**   **Cost:**

Equipment Name: **Cost:**

Equipment Name: **Cost:**

Expenses: **Cost:** 1,000

Total Estimated Costs: 15,000

Approved by Client: _____

Date: _____

Writing client proposals

For some projects, where you find yourself in a competitive situation you may have to bid for the work you propose to carry out. In such circumstances you will have to present a formal written document to your potential client. So you will need to expand your initial terms of reference into a full proposal. To do this, you have to include all the sections covered in the terms of reference and add some additional information to enhance your final proposal.

Structure any proposal in a clear and logical manner. Where there are several clients involved in the final decision-making process try to identify and reflect their various needs in your proposal.

Helpful tip

Keep the time spent on drafting a client proposal in line with the size of the assignment on offer. Don't spend one week writing a proposal for a project that is likely to last a few days. You need to use your time effectively and focus your energies on proposals that offer best promise.

Submit your proposal to your client as a typed and narrative document. It must not be presented as a completed form. Use the same headings as in your initial terms of reference but expand each section to provide more detailed information.

For example:

- Enhance the boundary section by explaining the type of research or information gathering you will undertake. Who you will want to interview and how much time you will need to complete the work.

- Enhance the activity time chart by providing a description for each activity – indicating not only your responsibilities but also your client's.

- Specify the time and costs involved and the use of other internal/external consultants.

- Remember when planning activities to take into account factors such as holidays and the availability of clients and their staff. Agree any absences in advance with your client so as to avoid problems at a later stage.

- Finally, remember to check all your key facts and numbers.

Additional headings you should include in your proposal concern your:

Consulting Experience

This section outlines your professional expertise and competence to carry out the assignment. Include your previous experience in addressing similar projects or problems and also include your curriculum vitae. If you have a team that will be used for the project, include the details of your team's skills and experience.

Methodology

This section deals with your approach to tackling the project by describing in detail your approach or methodology. If you are involved in information technology or training consultancy you might describe your process for conducting your development cycle (linear or iterative) or training needs analysis.

Remember the whole basis of effective client management is to avoid possible problems by predicting them in advance and taking corrective action to ensure they do not arise. The golden rule is to never surprise your client.

Managing initial meetings checklist

The first stage in the internal consulting process involves establishing a working relationship with your client. The primary objective is to clearly identify your client's needs and begin exploring how you might provide assistance. It involves submitting a terms of reference and agreeing in detail a project's objectives, time-scales and costs.

Questions you should ask:

- What does the client consider to be the problem?

- Do they appear to fully understand the problem and issues surrounding it?

- Has your client appeared to identify the right or wrong problem?

- Does your client want to take full ownership for the problem?

- Is your client aware of their limitations in trying to solve the problem?

- Does your client see you as a partner in tackling the problem?

- Are there other important parties or clients who may need to be brought into the project to ensure a successful outcome?

- Do they have the backing of their boss to start the project or do they have to sell it upwards?

- Is your client fully aware of their commitments and responsibilities in commissioning the project?

- What is the real problem facing your client?

Client's perspective of you:

- Are you competent and knowledgeable?

- Do you appear and behave in a professional manner?

- Can I work with you and trust you?

- Do you make me think in different ways about the problem?

- Do you have the right expertise and track record?

- Are your initial thoughts and plans practical and realistic?

- Is your terms of reference or proposal reasonable?

Other client thoughts:

- Do you report to other senior people within the organization?

- Do you listen well?

- Are you aloof or arrogant?

- Do you value my time?

- Do I like you as a person?

Other statements/questions you might use:

- What are your main business concerns at the moment?

- What are the real issues or problems as you see them?

- What will happen if the situation continues?

- What have other people said about the situation?

- What do your colleagues think about the situation?

- Why have you asked us to provide some assistance?

- What role do you see us playing in helping you address the problem?

- If we were successful with this project what would success look like?

- Could we have access to the relevant data and reports?

- Have you considered these other options...?

- Are there any parts of the organization or areas you do not want us to get involved in?

- Have you thought about any other ways that you might address the issue?

- These are our initial thoughts about tackling the work.

CHAPTER FIVE

Understanding and defining
the client's problem

FIVE
Understanding and defining the client's problem

Once your initial terms of reference or proposal has been agreed by your client you have to really begin to understand your client's problem. This requires a detailed, analytical review of the issues or circumstances surrounding the problem. In defining any business problem you need to maintain a clear and independent perspective at all times. Don't be prejudiced by past experiences or easily persuaded by emotive arguments or persuasive people. Maintaining a detached and objective outlook is essential to your success.

In understanding your client's problem endeavour to gather information from a variety of individuals and sources. Information on consultancy projects is normally collected through five key methods:

1 Desk research

2 Interviews

3 Group interviews

4 Questionnaires

5 Process mapping techniques

In this chapter we explore the essential characteristics of each and provide some key advice on how to use them to secure benefit for your client projects. Two key factors that will help you determine the most appropriate methods to use are, firstly, the number of people you can reasonably expect to involve given any time constraints and secondly, the depth of knowledge you need to fully understand the problem. Figure 11 illustrates the relationship of these two factors to the different approaches.

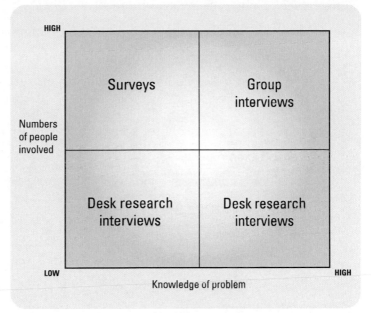

FIGURE 11: INFORMATION GATHERING TECHNIQUES

Desk research

In most cases desk research is conducted in the early stages of a project, although there may be circumstances where it will be required during the middle of a project. Desk research involves the identification and analysis of specific sources of documentary evidence that maybe relevant to your project. Of course there are lots of projects where any desk research is limited to reading up on some background papers or documents such as previous reports. But there may be other times where you will need to access a wide variety of information sources in preparation for the start of a project. In all situations you will need to apply a disciplined and analytical approach to your work so as to identify the relevant sources of information and record the key points for your future project work.

Desk research normally involves three stages:

1 Identification of relevant sources of information.

2 Review and analysis of the information sources.

3 Preparation of key findings and conclusions resulting from the research.

It may require you to review these sources of information:

- Organization reports

- Procedures and operating manuals

- Competitor publications

- Financial reports

- Technical journals

- Professional association reports and journals

- Trade journals

- Specialist journals

- Business magazines

- Government reports

- Consultancy surveys and reports

- Industry association reports

- Relevant books

Desk research helps build up a real understanding of a particular issue. In some cases it may result in you producing a report highlighting your key findings as part of the wider project being undertaken.

Interviewing clients

Preparing your interview structure

The first point to emphasis when interviewing people during the course of any project or assignment, is that everyone is a client; or they have the potential to become a client. It is therefore important to always conduct yourself with the utmost courtesy and professionalism; even when interviewing people who are in extreme circumstances unhelpful or even impolite. Treat everyone with equal respect. As an internal consultant you can never predict when you might end up working for someone you have interviewed. So always exercise care when conducting interviews. To upset or annoy someone today may not be a problem, but next year when you stand before them trying to secure a new piece of work it will be a different matter.

Any interview is a simple way of gaining information through questioning and discussion. Client interviews must be controlled by the consultant and have a clear set of objectives and structure. At the same time the interview must not give the impression of being an interrogation. To harass people over questions will only antagonise and result in negative outcomes.

Also be sure to avoid allowing any personality conflicts or personal likes and dislikes to cloud your judgement during an interview. Stay detached and objective at all times.

In preparing for interviews develop a checklist of all the issues you want to discuss. A broad range of questions will tend to be more helpful than a detailed list. The questions you will ultimately ask will depend on the replies and reactions you receive as the interview progresses. Be flexible in your approach. Having a checklist of questions provides you with more scope to adjust the focus and flow of your interview.

The key objective of any information gathering interview is to get your client talking. Again use the magical 80:20 Pareto rule; with your client speaking for 80% of the time and you asking questions for the remaining 20%. If you dominate an interview it is likely that you will leave it not having understood your client's viewpoint or, even worse, their problem. Your ability to listen rather than talk is critical. The most successful client interviews are those where you simply use a small but select number of open-ended questions and your client provides all the relevant information. A bad interview is where you do the talking for most of the time. That is the sign that you are operating as the expert consultant.

Your behaviour during the initial stages will tend to determine the level of trust that will exist throughout the interview. You therefore need to display lots of interest and empathy with your client. Accelerate this process by offering to share control of the interview and jointly agreeing the agenda.

At the interview's beginning you will need to establish your credibility as well as deal with any anxieties the client may have about the process. If you appear worried or nervous you can sometimes arouse similar tensions in less confident interviewees.

There is no need to present a highly detailed explanation of your technical qualifications and career details as this can be interpreted by some clients as demonstrating a lack of confidence or, even worse, arrogance. Your objective should be to instil in the client a sense of comfort and mutual respect. So keep it simple and state who you are, your role, some general background to the interview and your objectives for the meeting.

In developing and planning your interview approach keep to the following guidelines:

- Analyse in advance any background information on your client's operation, e.g. problem areas, performance indicators, key personalities, current business challenges, competitor threats.

- State clearly your aims and objectives for the interview.

- Decide on the topics you want to focus on – preferably with the aid of a checklist.

- Prepare and then plan your interview structure.

- Allocate timings for each section of your interview.

- Find out and agree with your client where the interview will take place. As a general rule people are more comfortable in their own surroundings. They will also have easy access to any additional information you may require.

- When making an interview appointment with clients always confirm the purpose and objectives of the meeting.

- Ideally write to them in advance of any interview to confirm the details. Enclose a draft agenda for the meeting. This helps to offset any concerns they may have about the interview and it also helps prepare them to deal with the issues you want to discuss.

- Refer to your written agenda during the interview and use it as a means of controlling the pace of your interview. It will help you to move the client forward if they are staying too long on one subject area.

- If you are interviewing together with a colleague make sure you agree clear roles beforehand. Allocate questions or specific topic areas to each other. Give your client a professional impression and show that you both have strong roles in the project. Having one consultant sitting and not asking any questions for an entire interview does little to instil client confidence. Even worse it could give the impression that you are wasteful and inefficient.

- Agree with your client that there will be no interruptions to the interview.

Insight

Internal consultants always try to 'Hunt in Pairs.'

Interviewing client alone can be difficult as it is very easy to get locked into a pattern of discussion and not realise that you have lost track or control. By working with another colleague you can develop specific roles and help each other if one of you gets into difficulties.

Hunting in pairs also helps when reviewing the interview afterwards.

Managing the client interview

At the start of any interview outline the purpose of the interview and again check the interviewee's understanding of the objectives. Even if you have previously sent a written confirmation to a client it maybe the case that they did not read it properly or they have forgotten about it. After having indicated the time you require for the interview politely request the assistance and agreement of the interviewee to your objectives. Ask your client whether they wish to add anything to the interview agenda. These formal courtesies may seem a little elaborate but they do help overcome any potential hostility that might in some instances be surrounding a project

Your questioning technique should allow your client to follow their own line of thought provided they do not move too far away from the areas you want to focus on. Be conscious of any time constraints that you or your client maybe working under. Remember that people are likely to disclose more when they feel comfortable and free to express themselves. Adopting an aggressive questioning stance is not necessary and will only result in your interviewee becoming antagonised and refusing to offer any real information. Also avoid interrupting or being overly critical of anything they may say. You may need to challenge them on some points but you can do this without adopting a hostile questioning technique.

At the end of your interview summarise what the client has stated and thank them for their help and co-operation. Also request permission to come back to them for additional information should your work require it.

Insight

A professional way to end an interview is to ask your client:

'Is there anything that we have not discussed or raised that you think maybe relevant to the work we are undertaking?'

In most cases you will get a neutral response but on some occasions you will get some really important piece of information that will help your overall project.

Equally this question has the nice effect of handing over the close of the interview to your client.

Managing client interviews – a checklist of good practice

- Make your client feel comfortable – put them at ease by a clear introduction.

- Ensure your client is clear about the objectives for the interview.

- Obtain your client's agreement to your objectives.

- Allow the client to add to the scope of the interview if they wish.

- Ask for permission to take notes during the interview.

- State how you intend to handle issues of confidentiality – being open and honest will help you establish rapport and trust.

- Outline what will happen with the information you are collecting.

- Encourage your client to do most of the talking.

- Use open-ended questions at the beginning of the interview.

- Follow-up client answers by using probing questions that elicit more details about issues..

- Confirm your understanding of what has been said by summarising regularly.

- Try not to be drawn into making specific comments on controversial issues and do not align yourself to any one viewpoint.

- Never criticise other people or departments.

ALSO DON'T FORGET TO:

- Keep on track with your interview structure.

- Ensure all your topic areas are covered.

- Ask for information on any new issues that emerge during the interview.

- Obtain specific examples, details or facts of what your client is trying to explain.

- Recognise irritation on the part of your client.

- Thank your interviewee for their time and assistance.

- Advise them about what will happen next.

THINGS TO AVOID DURING INFORMATION GATHERING INTERVIEWS:

- Talking too much at your client.

- Unnecessary jargon – it irritates clients and provides some with a ready opportunity to criticise you or your work; if not during the interview then almost certainly later with their colleagues.

- Interrupting your client.

- Making assumptions about the interviewee's views or opinions – check out or challenge all assumptions.

- Asking leading or multiple questions.

- Antagonising your client through aggressive behaviour.

- Running out of time.

Taking interview notes

Information that is obtained during any interviews should be recorded during the interview. Most consultants have to work hard at improving the quality of their note-taking. It can be a difficult task to take precise and detailed notes during a lengthy interview and you will need to develop a disciplined approach so as not to end up with pages of scribbled and semi-intelligible comments. Firstly record the name and role of the interviewee and the date on which the interview took place. At first this sounds obvious but again it is amazing how after you have interviewed perhaps twenty-five people, you look at a set of notes and wonder whose comments they belong to. The combined use of your broad list of questions and topic headings should assist you in structuring the information as the interview proceeds.

You will also need to review the information you obtain to check that it provides you with what you require to carry out your investigation or research. Clearly, the disciplined and analytical approach involved in collecting information is equally necessary in recording it.

Actions to take after an interview

- Write down a full account of the interview as soon as possible.

- Send a copy of your interview notes to the interviewee so that they can check and correct any misunderstandings or, alternatively, add any relevant points that may have been missed. This makes for clear communications and also presents a thorough and professional image.

Group interviews

Group interviews involve situations where for efficiency or operational concerns you decide to interview a group of people for your project. In some situations you may be faced with a group of production workers taking an extended lunch-break to accommodate your project schedule. Alternatively, you maybe asked to interview a group of managers at the end of one of their regular review meetings. In many respects the basic requirements of handling these types of interviews are the same as one-to-one situations.

However, you do need to be aware that in certain circumstances there may be requirements to ensure everyone has an equal contribution and that the discussions are not dominated by the more forceful or dominant members of the group. To that extent you may need to exercise strong control. One way that you can do this is to introduce the concept of ground-rules to guide peoples' behaviour during the discussions. Five simple but powerful examples are shown overleaf.

Ground rules for controlling group interviews

1 **Only one person speaks at a time** – a basic discipline, but one that often needs to be enforced in group situations to avoid several discussions taking place at once.

2 **People can agree to disagree** – this helps you move the discussion forward if it appears to be getting bogged down between a minority of participants.

3 **It is OK to be negative but try to also offer positive alternative solutions or ideas to address the problem** – this can help you manage people to be positive in their attitude. In some situations a group interview can degenerate into a negative spiral unless they are managed properly.

4 **Hierarchy is left at the door** – this can be helpful if you are having to manage a cross-section of people and believe there maybe concerns about status influencing peoples' views.

5 **Let's be hard on the issue and soft on the people** – this rule helps you focus people on getting to issues concerning problem areas rather than allowing personal recriminations to take place which can often happen in heated situations.

As the consultant, introduce these ground-rules at the outset of the group meeting and state that they are there to help ensure a productive exchange of views. Having introduced them it is essential that you police them during the meeting in order to derive the real benefit.

Using structured frameworks to obtain information

In group situations involving larger groups of say, 12 or more people you may consider introducing some structured group work to solicit everyone's views. To do this you might break them up into groups of 4-6 people and task them with discussing a set of specific questions and reporting back. In these types of situation you might typically use the classic SWOT analysis that requires a review of the Strengths, Weaknesses, Opportunities and Threats of a particular situation.

Figure 12 illustrates the SWOT framework.

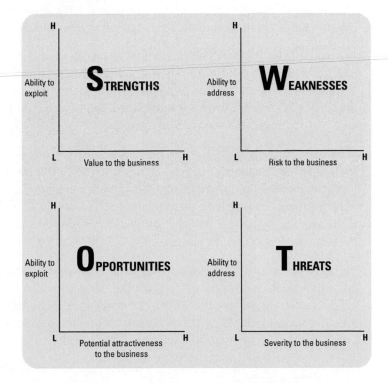

FIGURE 12: USING A SWOT ANALYSIS TO GATHER AND ASSESS INFORMATION

After having introduced the framework you would instruct small groups of people to spend 20-30 minutes producing their SWOT analysis on how they viewed a specific problem or situation. As the internal consultant you would then ask someone from each group to present back their analysis. You can lead a general discussion to clarify your understanding of what is being presented.

Once an overview of the SWOT analysis has been presented you can use some additional and very powerful questions to promote further discussion, e.g. What is the risk or severity of that weakness/threat actually happening? If we did invest more in that strength, what business benefit would it derive? Often these questions help provide greater focus on the key issues surrounding a problem.

Remember also that the SWOT analysis is a really useful and simple structure to conduct one-to-one interviews. You can simply keep asking a client to highlight the strengths and weaknesses etc until they are complete. You also have an easy way to collate your interview notes.

Another analytical tools that can be easily used in group situations is the forcefield analysis. This requires highlighting a particular problem or objective and then asking people to brainstorm or relate their experiences to the issue. In using the framework you have to direct peoples' thoughts and discussions into two distinct areas.

The driving or forcing factors are those that people believe are capable of helping solve the problem or achieving the objective. In contrast the blockers or obstacles are those factors that people believe are currently preventing the problem being addressed or the objective being achieved.

When structuring these exercises, provide people with flipcharts and working papers including 'post-it' notes to help them build up the information. The power of both the

SWOT and forcefield models are their ability to display a lot of potentially complex information in a simple visual format.

Figure 13 provides a simple outline of the forcefield approach.

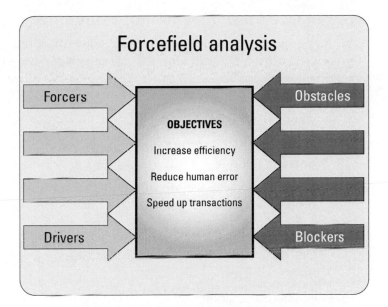

FIGURE 13: FORCEFIELD ANALYSIS

Both frameworks also enable people to present their views and opinions in a structured and focused way. This means you are also able to collect information in an efficient and controlled manner.

They are also an effective means of recording the outcomes of a meeting as each group will have presented their views on flip-chart paper. This means the data can be easily typed up and edited.

Both frameworks are also very simple to explain and highly participative in their approach. Two essential ingredients to getting the best out of any group interview situation.

Types of interview questioning techniques

With your overall interview objectives already in mind there are several types of questioning technique you can use to collect information. Begin at the outset of any interview considering whether you are trying to:

- Obtain hard facts?
- Clarify your understanding of a process, issue or problem?
- Get your interviewee to comment on an idea or proposition?
- Challenge your interviewee's thinking?
- Understand the attitudes and feelings surrounding an issue?
- Assess the interviewee?

Once you have answered these questions you can then employ a wide range of techniques to elicit client responses. Developing confidence with these questions and techniques will come naturally as you gain more experience of interviewing people. In the early days of your consulting work, experiment with these techniques and don't be too worried if on certain occasions they do not always produce the desired results. Interviewing is a skill that develops over time.

Using open-ended questions

Open-ended questions are an essential element in any consultant's interview toolkit as they prevent your client providing simple one word replies. Open-ended questions encourage people to talk and are particularly helpful during the initial stages of an interview, as they promote positive rapport and dialogue.

Open-ended questions are also highly effective in either introducing new topics or probing for more detailed information on a particular subject.

The most powerful open-ended questions begin with: **What? Why? When? How? Where?** and **Who?**

Examples of open-ended questions

- What was actually happening at that point...?
- How would you describe the current situation?
- What are the current facts as regards service levels?
- What are the performance figures relating to the system?
- What were the objections raised by the customer?
- Where is the unit at this present point in time?
- When was the discrepancy first identified?
- What do you see as the three major issues facing your operation?
- Why did that situation remain in place for so long?
- How are the current systems managed?
- How would you describe the current strengths of the operation?
- Who had the primary responsibility?

- When did the situation begin to worsen?

- When did management realise that the project was beginning to slip?

- What other issues have contributed to the problem?

- When did you realise customers were reacting badly?

- What would 'Y' be expected to do in such situations?

Open-ended questions can also be used to understand your clients' views and opinions on specific issues, e.g:

- How do you feel about…?

- What do you think about…?

- What do you think of the idea that…?

- What are your views on…?

- How important are… would you say?

- What alternatives are available?

- How would you react if…?

Using specific questions

Specific questions allow you to probe for and obtain specific details or facts surrounding an issue. In many cases you want to emerge from an interview with not just opinions but also lots of hard facts. Specific questions help get the details. Use them to follow up on open-ended questions. Some examples are:

- When exactly did that situation first arise?

- Who is responsible for or owns that process?

- When did the breakdown first happen?

- Why did the operator report the incident to you first?

- What were the exact circumstances involved?

- What was the agreed conclusion to those discussions?

- What was the percentage increase at that time?

- How was the report presented to the management?

- Did anyone query the specification the first time it was announced?

Linking questions

The link question is a variation of the open-ended question. It acts as a bridge and allows you to make a transition from one question to another, thus promoting a smooth interview flow. Examples of link questions include:

- You mentioned just now that..., how did this affect...?

- We've just discussed..., could we now have a look at another element of the system problem...?

- How does that issue relate to the point you raised earlier concerning the financing problems...?

- Is there a relationship between the quality and level of training being given?

- As you finished talking about product x it brings to mind some questions I have that relate to product y. How strong a product is that?

Exploring and validating alternative approaches

During certain interviews and, more particularly, during the later stages of a project you may need to begin validating certain hypotheses, strategies or actions. Using the following questions can help you obtain reactions from interested parties or clients. The skill is to suggest the idea or proposition but not sound as though you have already reached a conclusion, as this may put your client off from giving a clear and unbiased answer. You want your client to give you a straightforward reaction to the proposition or proposal.

- Perhaps we could do it another way – such as…?

- Is this the only option available? – What about the xy approach? Would that work?

- What about taking a radically different approach such as…?

- Can we look at it this way…How about integrating all the activities together?

- Next time could we complete the job using…?

- What if your competitors did the opposite and started pursuing the idea – would that suggest it could be made to work?

- I am told that with sufficient resources the process can produce those results – what are your thoughts?

Providing non-verbal encouragement during interviews

Non-verbal encouragement involves you in making noises such as: 'Ah?', 'Oh?', 'Uhh?', 'Hmm?' as your client talks. This is a rapport building technique that lets your client know that you are actively listening and that you would like to hear more. Verbal acknowledgements are indications of attention and when combined with appropriate facial expressions (smiles, raised eyebrows, etc.) they encourage your client to talk further.

Similarly, you can also show empathy to your client by the careful use of body posture, facial expressions and eye contact. Leaning forward and demonstrating expressions of interest promotes increased dialogue. However, be careful not to overplay these techniques as some clients may find them off-putting or even manipulative.

Using supportive statements

Supportive statements involve phrases such as: 'I see...?', 'And then what happened...?', 'That's interesting...' 'Could you say a little bit more about that, it sounds very relevant.'

Supportive statements produce the same results as non-verbal encouragement – an extended answer from your client that reduces the need for a set of further detailed questions. The aim in using supportive statements is to lead your client into providing as much information and detail as possible with the least amount of spoken comment from you.

Checking your facts and asking for specific information

Throughout an assignment and during any interview you will need to establish specific facts or obtain key information. This requires a more direct questioning approach but be careful to ensure that you do not sound hostile towards people. The directness of the question can sometimes make this difficult. So when thinking about such questions consider your voice tone, the sensitivity of the question and the timing of it. A too heavy handed approach and you may sound like an interrogator.

The following types of question illustrate the approach:

- Where did that information come from?

- Can you confirm those figures?

- Can you confirm that you do actually report to the Operations Director?

- I have been shown a separate set of figures on… can you confirm their accuracy?

- So what is the current system's availability?

- Can you verify this data?

Simply by changing the tone of your voice you can significantly change the way these questions might be interpreted. So be careful and think how the client might react. Avoid being the proverbial bull in a china shop! A simple 'please' or 'would it be possible' can help to soften the blunt sounding nature of some of these questions.

Showing empathy with your client

At certain times you will need to demonstrate empathy with your client. This can be particularly important when your client is discussing sensitive issues and feeling vulnerable about relating particular details. The following statements can help you to get through these difficult areas of an interview:

- You are really concerned about this, aren't you?

- I can see this has caused you a great deal of concern.

- It is pretty obvious from what you have said, why you were annoyed...

- I can understand how you must have felt about the situation.

- That must have been a really difficult situation to deal with.

In other situations you may need to offer some kind of support or assistance to your client in order to engage their continued support and interest. In which case the following statements can be helpful:

- Yes, it is irritating, but let me see if I can help...

- You are quite right to be angry, but I can suggest some ideas for resolving the issue...

- There is every reason to feel upset, but have you thought about...

- Can you tell me the details, I may be able to...

Key word repetition

Key word repetition is another rapport building technique that encourages your clients to offer more information on a particular issue. It simply requires you to pick up on a key word and reflect it back to your client in the following manner:

Client   'For two years I've been working on systems design.'

Internal Consultant   'Oh, systems design...'

When 'Oh, systems design,' is phrased with a questioning inflection of voice tone this can often be sufficient to prompt the client to explain a lot more about the subject. Key word repetition is another technique that again allows you to operate with an economy of questions.

Using the pause

Some people don't like the sound of silence when inter-viewing. But remember that immediately rushing in with another question to avoid a momentary silence can result in a client failing to offer an important piece of information. If you want your client to continue talking and add to what they have said, a strong pause can stimulate this as effec-tively as any spoken question. A pause provides your interviewee with a chance to think, re-phrase or add to any preceding answers. The judicious use of the pause is one of the most powerful techniques to employ in an interview. Developing a strong capability in the use of pauses will reap real benefits.

As Mark Twain once wrote:

'The right word may be effective but no word was ever as effective as a rightly timed pause.'

Using summaries

Use summaries regularly throughout any interview. They allow you to check your understanding of any facts that you have been given and to clarify your client's thoughts on important issues. Summary statements also provide you with another method of achieving a smooth change of direction from one topic to another during an interview

Summary questions prevent your client drifting from your interview agenda and allow you to regain control without an abrupt interruption. To that extent they are very helpful in controlling talkative clients.

Summary statements involve phrases such as:

- As I have understood the situation what you are saying is that...

- So what you're saying is... Is that correct?

- If I have understood you correctly... Now could we move on to discuss...

- So, to summarise you are saying that more work will be required to get the project back on track.

Dealing with mistakes

You must expect to make mistakes in some interviews about some issue or information; it is inevitable. The best advice is to openly admit that you have made a mistake to your client, offer an apology and move on. Trying to cover up the issue or avoid it will only make things worse. If this happens try using the following statements:

Sorry that is my mistake!

You're right, I got it wrong I do apologise.

That's quite right, I should have realised... please accept my apologies.

I apologise for the misunderstanding on that issue.

Counter-productive questions

Any question that detracts from the smooth flow of an interview might be called counter-productive. Classic examples include:

Multiple questions

Multiple questions combine several questions into one long statement. The result is to add confusion to the interview process and allow your client to be selective in their answer. Invariably clients fail to address all the questions that you posed.

- So how did you manage to achieve those results without impacting on other parts of the operation and how did your colleagues react?

- Why did you join this part of the organization and how does it compare to the other operation that you worked in, what do you see as the key weaknesses?

- So how long have you worked in this operation and do you like it or are there problems?

Leading questions

Another counter-productive question is the leading question that either invites a particular response or suggests a 'right' answer is required from the client. The leading question is often phrased in the form of an emotional or judgemental tone such as:

- You've got to admit that...?

- Isn't it a fact that...?

- You must concede that...?

- You will surely acknowledge...?

- You're not suggesting that...?

- You don't think that...?

In the case of some of the above examples, you maybe expecting the response 'Yes, of course!'. In others the appropriate answer may be 'No, of course not'. In either case you are suggesting to the client that you have an answer in mind and that you would like it confirmed. Of course there are some circumstances where this might prove an effective technique to test out someone's views or opinions. But be careful when applying such a potentially provocative approach.

Critical leading questions

The critical leading question relics on a stronger degree of implied criticism or judgement when posing the question. In some ways it is simply a stronger version of the leading question.

- Surely you can't believe that…, can you?
- You don't really think that… do you?
- Surely you're not suggesting that…?
- You don't honestly think that…, do you?
- You cannot for one minute, believe your competition would ever do that, do you?

Any response other than a strong rejection of the question might imply a lack of credibility on the part of your client. This form of questioning can therefore frequently appear antagonistic and so also provoke a negative client reaction. This type of question should be avoided unless you feel that your client relationship would not be damaged by such a strong approach.

Using questionnaires to gather information

Whilst interviews allow you to question people in depth on specific issues, questionnaires make it possible for you to assess the views of a large number of people relatively quickly and cheaply. The use of a questionnaire can be a very efficient way to gather information from a wide group of people. Questionnaires also introduce a degree of quantitative data into any analysis. The ability to build a quantitative database of evidence can be vital on projects where peoples' views and opinions are involved. Arguments supported by statements such as '70% of managers agree' are always useful in influencing clients.

Questionnaires can of course be used on a wide number of projects involving staff and customer surveys, reactions to new IT systems and other organizational improvements. So understanding the steps involved in designing and administering a questionnaire can be extremely useful. Whilst it is possible to develop a questionnaire without too much difficulty there are some rules that you should observe. Figure 14 illustrates a broad overview of the questionnaire design process.

Designing a questionnaire

The questionnaire design process can be divided into a series of nine key steps:

Step 1: Identifying your questionnaire themes by interviewing people.

Step 2: Arranging initial interviews.

Step 3: Preparing key themes for your interviews.

Step 4: Conducting interviews.

Step 5: Identifying key issues.

Step 6: Preparing and reviewing questions.

Step 7: Producing your draft questionnaire.

Step 8: Reviewing your draft questionnaire with your client.

Step 9: Conducting the survey with your completed questionnaire.

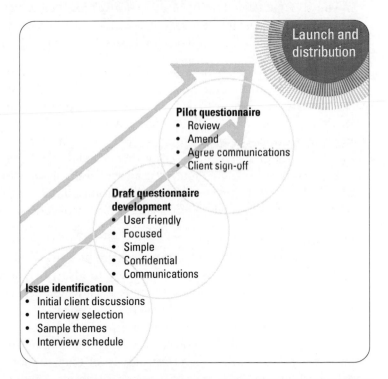

FIGURE 14: GATHERING INFORMATION – THE QUESTIONNAIRE PROCESS

Step 1: Identifying questionnaire themes by interviewing people

The first step in designing any questionnaire is to agree with your client the number of people who will be interviewed so that you can identify the key themes or issues to be included in your survey.

There are no specific rules as to the number of people that you should interview. But you will need to ensure that you include a cross-section of people who will ultimately appear in your final survey. This ensures that any views or issues that reflect different interest groups will emerge in you interviews and so find a place in your final questionnaire design.

One important decision that you will have to make is whether to interview people individually or in groups. Normally, senior managers prefer to be interviewed on their own, but it is also of course possible to interview people effectively in small groups. The group approach saves both time and money although as we have earlier discussed it can sometimes be operationally difficult to manage. You will need to discuss the various practical and operational implications of these approaches with your client before proceeding.

One further issue involves selecting the right people for your interviews. In our experience it is better if you draw up a list of names and then discuss their suitability with your client. Because the people you select may not always be readily available you should agree a clear basis on which you can select alternatives. To save time, it is preferable that you agree with your client that you can approach substitutes for interview without having to constantly refer back to them, unless of course there are operational constraints. You will also need to check that your client provides a representative sample of people so that you get a balanced and realistic set of views and not just those that your client wants you to hear. So, if in doubt, make sure you challenge some of your client's decisions.

Step 2: Arranging initial interviews

You will need to compose and circulate a letter in advance of your interviews explaining the purpose and objectives of the exercise. Your letter should also detail the date, time and location of the interview and identify the topic areas you want to discuss. You should also thank people in advance for agreeing to participate in the exercise and express your wish to minimise any operational disturbance that your visit might bring. You should schedule interviews for between 1.5 and 2 hours depending upon the type of survey you are conducting, and you should be able to hold 4 to 6 interview sessions per day.

Step 3: Preparing key themes for your interviews

Before conducting your interviews, you will need to draw up a list of possible topics and issues for discussion. You will have already discussed and agreed these with your client in advance of any interview programme. As we stated in our interview section, this list of themes should only be used as an outline and prompt, rather than as a detailed check-list to be followed rigorously. It will then help provide a focus and structure to your interviews and ensure a smooth flow.

Step 4: Conducting interviews

During this stage you try to keep on schedule and hope that you do not experience any last minute cancellations. You will also need to maintain your discipline in recording information during the interviews. Any spare time between interviews should be used writing up your interview notes and planning ahead.

Step 5: Identifying key issues

From your interview notes, you must then develop a summary of the issues raised by people. You need to document the location, department or function of the people involved and a short paragraph describing the various issues raised. In lots of cases you will have confirmed the issues already identified during your earlier client discussions. You will however need to review these issues with your client when preparing the final questionnaire as the chances are new issues will have emerged. For example, you may have identified from your interviews three recurring themes such as pay and rewards, staff moral and the restructuring plan. When you come to review these issues with your client you may find that only two of these issues need to be dealt with in the survey as the other will be the subject of a separate review. The end result is that you would have two key issues from which to begin developing your questionnaire. Your next action is to begin to shape your questionnaire content by preparing a set of questions for each theme.

Step 6: Preparing and reviewing questions

The following is a check-list that will help you prepare a set of questions. The most effective approach is to:

- Prepare questions for each issue that was raised.

- Add additional questions based on any other research you may have conducted.

- Brainstorm as many other relevant questions as you can.

- Refine your list, deleting questions that appear irrelevant, repetitive or redundant. Re-word others as appropriate. It is often necessary to draft questions three of four times before arriving at a final draft questionnaire.

- Check that you have the right balance of negative and positive questions.

- Make sure the questions are understandable. Keep them simple and clear.

- Make sure people have the necessary knowledge or experience to answer the questions accurately.

ASK SPECIFIC QUESTIONS

General questions should not be used when specific answers are required. For example:

> *'Are you satisfied with the IT Help Desk response?'*

This is not a good question if what you really want to find out is how quickly the IT Help Desk responds when a phone call is made. So a better question to ask would be:

> *'Does the IT Help Desk pick up phone calls in less than 3 rings?'*

AVOID AMBIGUOUS QUESTIONS

Ambiguous questions allow people the opportunity to provide different interpretations to the same question, and so produce meaningless results.

For example:

> *'Do you often work overtime because of lack of administrative support?'*

If the answer to this question was 'No', then what does it actually mean?

> *'No, I do not often work overtime'*

or

> *'No, I do not lack administrative support'*

You can see that questions like this leave you open to criticism at the feedback stage. So be clear about what it is you are trying to measure or assess.

USE PRECISE WORDING

Words such as 'fairly', 'generally', 'often', 'many' and 'appropriate' should be avoided as you will then tend to generate inconsistent responses from different people. What is 'fairly good support' for one person is poor support to another.

AVOID LEADING QUESTIONS

Questions should be presented in a neutral way so as to prevent the manipulation of a desired response. An example of a leading question is:

'Do you feel your hard work is appreciated?'

The way to avoid the inherent bias that this type of question can produce is to introduce a number of questions around the central theme of reward that can then be collectively analysed. For example:

'On average, I work more than 40 hours each week'

'My salary is below the national average for the job I do'

'My manager gives me praise when I do a good job'

Leading questions can also be caused by a failure to state alternatives. For example:

'Do you prefer working for a manager of your own sex?'

instead of:

'Would you rather work for a man or a woman, or doesn't it matter?'

KEEP QUESTIONS SHORT

Long questions should be kept to a minimum as they reduce the amount of time people need to spend completing the questionnaire. This reduces any sense of irritation or possible misunderstanding on the part of the person completing the document.

CAREFUL PHRASING

Never ask a question that will put someone on the defensive or make them feel in the wrong. Questions that people find rude or inconsiderate may not only affect their reply, but may also affect their response to the survey as a whole. Also, always remember to avoid jargon and abbreviations unless it is clear that people understand what they mean.

Step 7: Producing your draft questionnaire

Having prepared your questions you will then need to begin the process of structuring your questionnaire format and the first key issue to address is the response scale that you will use.

RESPONSE FORMAT – LIKERT SCALE

The most favoured format to use for your questionnaire response is the Likert Scale see figure 15 overleaf. This involves asking someone whether they agree or disagree with a statement by indicating on a scale their strength of agreement or disagreement. There are usually five basic responses:

- Strongly Disagree
- Disagree
- Uncertain/No Opinion/Don't Know
- Agree
- Strongly Agree

There should be an equal number of alternating positive and negative worded questions in your questionnaire so as to avoid any potential bias. The advantage of a Likert Scale is that it measures the strength of an attitude or belief whilst at the same time being easy for people to complete.

Characteristics of the HR Function		Strongly disagree	Disagree	Neither agree or disagree	Agree	Strongly agree
1	Seeks involvement with line managers in formulating business strategy and policy and in the planning process	1	2	3	4	5
2	Develops and implements coherent and integrated HR policies in support of business plans	1	2	3	4	5
3	Creates and conveys a clear view of HR aims and objectives, and the steps necessary to achieve them	1	2	3	4	5
4	Learns about activities/processes that form the basis of the internal customers business; uses this to improve service delivery	1	2	3	4	5
5	Builds effective working relationships with internal customers characterised by trust and respect	1	2	3	4	5
6	Adapts policies, activities and behaviour to the needs of different business units and different situations	1	2	3	4	5
7	Understands those factors which influence business performance	1	2	3	4	5

FIGURE 15: AN EXAMPLE OF THE LIKERT SCALE ON A QUESTIONNAIRE

RESPONSE FORMAT – FREE FORM REPLIES

Free form replies are open-ended questions that allow people to write what they want on a subject. You should generally avoid structuring the questionnaire so that a free form reply is needed to answer each question. This is because:

- A significant amount of time is needed by people to answer these questions and it is likely this time and effort will reduce the overall response rate to your questionnaire. People will simply get fed up writing or not bother at all.

- Those who write the most will inevitably exert more influence on the results.

- Collecting and analysing the responses is very time consuming.

- There are many difficulties in analysing and presenting the replies in a structured and systematic way as people will tend to write what they want and you end up with lots of diverse information which is difficult to present back to your client.

SECTION AT THE END

However, free form replies can yield useful information. So for many surveys, it may be a good idea to include a section at the end of your questionnaire that invites people to add any comments without presenting a specific question for them to answer. This has the advantage of allowing people to raise issues that they feel strongly about and which have not been covered by the questionnaire. We have included this type of approach in our organizational survey in the toolkit chapter at the end of this book. You will see that it combines both the free form reply approach with a Likert scale.

However, analysis of such data should be treated with caution. It is likely that only a relatively small proportion of people will make additional comments and these will not necessarily be representative of the whole group of people being surveyed.

Nevertheless, you will generate some useful comments that you may find valuable in your client feedback stage.

USING CHECKLIST RESPONSES

Checklist responses are a good method to use where you need to collect responses to a question other than agreement or disagreement. An example of a checklist format is:

'I work the following hours on my computer each day:'

- Less than 1 hour ☐
- 1-3 hours ☐
- More than 3 hours ☐

NUMBERS OF QUESTIONS

Your questionnaire should be no longer than is absolutely necessary to achieve its purpose. The temptation in questionnaire design is always to ask too many questions. Lengthy questionnaires are unlikely to be answered accurately or completely. In many situations an overly complex questionnaire will result in a low response rate. So keep things short and brief.

DEMOGRAPHIC DATA (PERSONAL DETAILS)

To analyse peoples' responses and identify different views without breaking confidentiality, it is normal on the front of your questionnaire, to ask people to categorise themselves according to their organization grade, location, department or any other item that you may have agreed with your client. You do however need to be careful that too detailed a breakdown will lead people to suspect that their individual responses can be identified and this might affect their replies.

COMPLETION TIME AND RETURN

The amount of time someone should take to complete your questionnaire should be explained on the first page of the questionnaire as part of your general instructions. People should not be asked to complete a questionnaire in too short a period of time as this may mean they will rush and not give accurate responses.

With regard to returning the questionnaire after completion you should set on average a target of ten working days from distribution to return. This should provide people with sufficient time and also give you time to manage the logistics surrounding the exercise. Avoid periods longer than ten days as this indicates a lack of urgency and priority in peoples' minds and will result in a weaker response rate.

QUESTIONNAIRE INSTRUCTIONS

You must provide clear instructions on how to complete the questionnaire. Use bold print and block capitals to emphasise key points and:

- Indicate how all the questions should be answered, for example, by circling, crossing or ticking the answers.

- Show what each category of response means, for example, 1 = Strongly Agree, 5 = Strongly Disagree.

- Tell people how to correct mistakes in their answers.

- Indicate the amount of time it should take to complete the questionnaire.

- Remind people to complete the Personal Details section and check that they have answered all the questions before returning the questionnaire.

- Clearly state who they should return the questionnaire to and by what date.

COVERING LETTER

Before finalising the content of your draft questionnaire you should prepare a letter to accompany it. This should contain the following information:

- The purpose of the questionnaire.

- Who has commissioned it.

- Why the individual has been selected to complete the questionnaire.

- The confidentiality agreements surrounding the results.

- Explain that there are no right or wrong answers.

- Explain what the next steps are.

- Thank people in advance for their co-operation.

Ideally, this letter should be signed off by the client or the lead project consultant. In projects where there is a lot of sensitivity it may be better for the consultant to sign it as it emphasises the issue of independence. In less sensitive circumstances it is a good idea to get the client to sign the letter as it demonstrates their commitment to the exercise.

QUESTIONNAIRE ADMINISTRATION

Do not under-estimate the amount of work needed to process the questionnaires when they are returned. Of course when dealing with numbers in excess of thirty you should use information technology to process the results. This will involve the answers from each questionnaire being typed (or preferably scanned where very large numbers are involved) into a computer using a suitable software package that will ultimately process the data and produce meaningful information. There are a few software packages that are designed to process questionnaires, however, many people use their favourite spreadsheet, database or statistical package. If you are not comfortable in dealing with this part of the process make sure you get the right people with the right skills to complete your data analysis. It is not an overly complex process but it does need to be carried out in a systematic manner and have lots of cross-checks built into the process to ensure the validity of the data.

Step 8: Reviewing your draft questionnaire with your client

Once you have reviewed your draft questionnaire with your client and agreed to the content and all the administrative arrangements surrounding the process, you then need to test it on a small number of between ten and twenty people to check that it is understandable. These people should be broadly representative of your final survey population. In selecting people for this process try to select those who will be conscientious and so inclined to comment and add value to the final questionnaire design.

In conducting this review ask the people involved to make a note of any difficult questions or confusing areas in the draft questionnaire. The feedback you will then receive will almost inevitably reveal flaws and problems with specific questions. The most common faults that are likely to emerge during this process are:

- Using technical or organization jargon that is not understood by people.

- Not using language or terminology that is familiar to people.

- Including repetitive questions.

- Inappropriate questions. For example, you will loose credibility if you ask a person who does not supervise others a question on how they get on with their staff.

- Assuming that people have a complete understanding of the organization. For example, employees may not understand the phrase 'The Operational Board'.

Of course not all the points raised may lead to changes but you will almost invariably need to change some aspects of the questionnaire.

Step 9: Conducting the survey with your finalised questionnaire

Once all the points that have been raised in your pilot questionnaire have been noted and reviewed, your client should be given the opportunity to add, change or remove any questions. You are now ready to send out your final questionnaire together with an accompanying letter.

You must make sure that all the administrative arrangements are in place and that the right people have been briefed about the exercise. The aim is to distribute your questionnaires as quickly as possible and to then obtain as many completed replies as fast as possible, and certainly within your project timescales so that you can then begin your analysis phase.

On large-scale surveys involving many hundreds of people you may want to set up some telephone help-lines to deal with any queries that people might have about the survey. But if you have planned everything out and communicated clearly there should be no major problems.

In presenting your survey feedback you should use graphical outputs of the type that can easily be generated by today's software packages. Figure 16 provides a simple example.

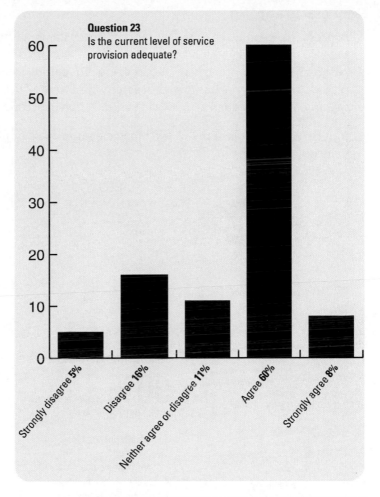

FIGURE 16: SURVEY FEEDBACK DISPLAYED GRAPHICALLY

The benefit of outputs like the one illustrated is that they immediately tell the story to clients and so are highly effective at communicating responses and indicating trends. Whilst you would need to back them up with a written report and detailed statistical data the power of a graphical presentation is so much greater than the written word.

Process mapping

Process mapping has a long tradition in the systems world but also developed wider interest during the 1990s amid the surge in business process re-engineering. Re-engineering projects reviewed core business processes with a view to identifying non-value added activities in organization processes.

Figure 17 illustrates some of the classic examples of non-valued added activity.

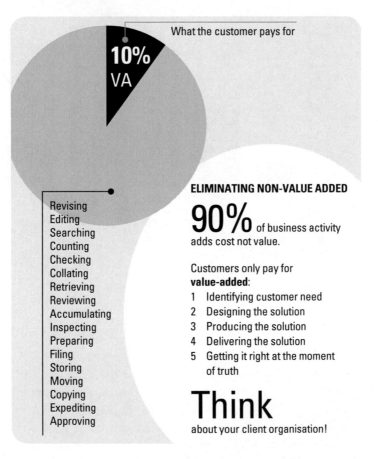

FIGURE 17: PROCESS THINKING AND VALUE ADDED

Whilst not a new concept, process mapping can be a very powerful way to build up a clear picture of how certain organizational processes work. To that extent it is a very useful method of collecting and gathering information about existing processes and work approaches. It is particularly relevant in re-organization and information technology projects that require a detailed understanding of existing operations.

At the heart of the process mapping technique is the use of classic systems tools to produce detailed process flow diagrams. Figure 18 highlights some of the more readily used symbols and illustrates how they can be used to describe the various elements of a work process.

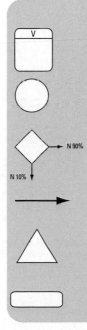

SOME CLASSIC PROCESS MAPPING DEFINITIONS

Activity rectangle
Used when no activity of any kind

Connector
Used to show information flows to or from another process chain

Decision points
Percent probability of each branch should be indicated

Direction of arrow flow
Denotes the direction and order of process steps

Queue
Shows where the object of the process waits, with no steps or actions taking place

Boundary
Indicates the beginning or end of a process

FIGURE 18: THE PROCESS TOOLKIT

The aim in using these symbols is to build up a clear picture as to the precise steps or actions involved in a specific process such as customer ordering or distribution. Process mapping can be used to build up an understanding of almost any part of an organization. As an approach it can generate powerful insights into the amount of time a process takes and how much value added time is involved. Indeed, once you start using these few symbols you will be surprised how easy it is to build up a detailed picture of a process. When applied in a re-engineering context, process mapping aims to assist in the identification and then removal of non-valued added activities so as to produce more efficient and leaner processes.

Figure 19 details how value added activities can be identified using a simple decision tree.

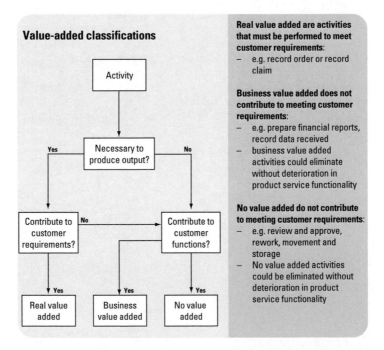

FIGURE 19: HOW TO CLASSIFY VALUE ADDED AND NON-VALUE ADDED

Of course the notion of what actually constitutes a value added process in an organization is often a controversial discussion. Nevertheless, the decision tree can help to pose the right questions for any review that you might be undertaking. Process mapping involves five key stages and begins with a series of interviews:

1 Interviewing job or process holders about what they actually do. This involves:

- Identifying critical or core processes

- Establishing the key steps and times to perform individual activities

- Identifying any wider organizational factors that might impact on the performance of the process

2 Translate interview information into an initial process map

3 Validate your process map with the process owner – check that you have understood everything:

- Identify value added and non-value added time in the process

- Confirm the existing process map:
  - Discuss findings with your client
  - Discuss findings with process holders

4 Redesign the process to improve the process or remove non-value added activities

5 Involve client and process holders

Process mapping builds up a clear and coherent picture of what is actually happening in parts of an organization.

Figures 20 shows the way in which various activities are mapped and then classified to generate a process map.

ACTIVTY DEFINITIONS

Class code	Definition	Classification
"V"	What the customer requires – must do to produce product or service	Value added
"Q"	Queue/wait state (not moving – idle)	Non value added
"I"	Inspection/approval (Ensuring activity is performed correctly)	Non value added
"M"	Transport, move (Moving from place to place)	Non value added
"P"	Preparation (Preparing to do work)	Non value added
"R"	Redundant (Unnecessary activity)	Non value added

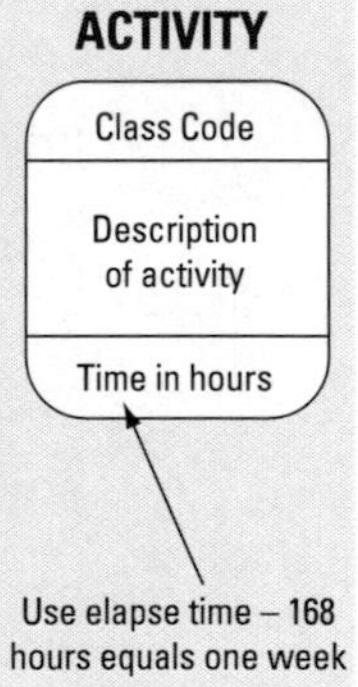

ACTIVITY

Class Code

Description of activity

Time in hours

Use elapse time – 168 hours equals one week

FIGURE 20: WHAT IS DRIVING PERFORMANCE?

The whole approach can help you build up a detailed understanding of processes and Figure 21 illustrates a simple example involving the steps involved in making a decision to go fishing. You can see how the various symbols are used to describe the key steps involved in this process and how significant this type of analysis can be made in reviewing organizations and their core processes.

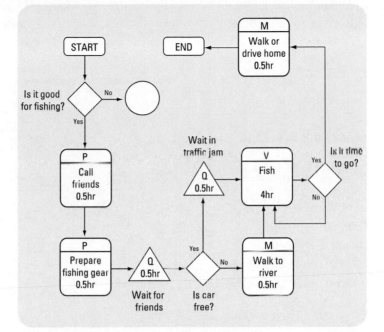

FIGURE 21: THIS IS HOW YOUR PROCESS MAPS SHOULD LOOK

In addition to developing process maps, another key element of the approach involves identifying wider organizational issues that might be impacting on the performance of a process. To obtain this type of information you will need to use lots of the approaches we have identified in our section on interviewing.

Figure 22 highlights some of the wider issues that may have to be considered in any major organization project. We will refer to more of these issues in our chapter involving change management. But it is essential that when undertaking any process review you also identify how the process fits into the wider organization. Processes do not work in isolation and you do need to consider other key organizational factors such as organization structure, rewards, skill levels, technological capabilities etc. Being able to identify how each process is influenced by such factors is key to any successful re-design initiative.

	Sales order process under review				
ORGANISATIONAL FACTORS Barrier or enabler (1 = enabler, 5 = barrier)	Develop new products	Process sales order	Prepare quotation	Close the contract	Overall impact on time, cost and quality
Culture/behaviours					
Organisation					
Processes/workflows					
Job design and responsibilities					
Skills and knowledge requirements					
Motivation/incentives					
Communications					
Operating procedures and policies					
Human resource management					
Technology					
Stakeholders					

FIGURE 22: PROCESS THINKING – WIDER ORGANIZATIONAL ANALYSIS

Whilst business process re-engineering achieved big performance improvements in many organizations, it did in the mid and late 1990's become the subject of much criticism. Many organizations applied the concepts in an overly simplistic way with the result that it became associated with many crude and brutal cost cutting exercises. The result was often failed projects with very poorly executed implementation strategies. A significant problem was that people failed to see these processes in the bigger organizational context.

This recent history and experience may mean that some people may view process mapping techniques negatively. Care will need to be exercised when selling in such an approach – remember your client may have a bad prior experience. When interviewing people on a process be very sensitive to their concerns about the aims and objectives of your work.

Despite these concerns the benefits that can result from process mapping can be considerable so add it to your toolkit of expertise.

Process analysis questions

Listed below are two sets of questions that you can employ when interviewing job or process holders. One identifies the detailed aspects of any process. The second set identifies any organizational factors that might be impacting on the performance of the process.

Process questions

- What are the inputs that start your process off?
- What are the functions or events that drive your process?
- Who are the suppliers (both internal and external) to your process?
- What are the outcomes or products of your process?
- Who are the ultimate customers of your process?
- What do you do next?
- Why do you then wait until x happens before completing that part of the process?

- Why do you record that information?

- What then happens to that information?

- Why do you have to refer that decision to x?

- Who uses the information you process?

- Can you describe the logical sequence of activities you perform to complete your process?

- How much time does each activity take to complete?

- How much queue (dead) time is there between activities?

Organizational issues questions

- How do your customers react to the responsiveness and quality of the outcomes of your process?

- What performance measures are in place to monitor the results of your process?

- What kinds of things prevent you from achieving better results in the process?

- Are there any other wider organizational issues that you feel need to be resolved to help you process better results?

- What factors annoy you about the way your department operates?

- If you had total freedom to improve the efficiency of your department what specific things would you do?

Understanding and defining your client's problem – being client focused

This stage of the consulting process involves the systematic collection of information in order to understand your client's underlying problem(s) and begin developing possible solutions.

Questions you should ask?

- How much detailed information do you need to collect?
- What information is already available within the organization?
- What other information will you need to collect?
- What research will you need to conduct?
- What methodologies will you need to use to collect information? – interviews, questionnaires, process mapping, observation etc.
- Whose involvement and support will you need?
- What sorts of costs will be involved in terms of time, logistics and finance?
- How will you handle the issue of confidentiality during your information gathering work. What commitments/agreements will you give to your client(s)? What will you say to interviewees? What will you tell them about the next steps?
- How will you present your findings? What report, presentation format will you use and to what sort of client audience will you ultimately present?
- How are people around the organization going to react to the project and to it's aims?
- Are there any 'political' issues surrounding this project that you need to be aware of?

Client's perspective of you:

- Do you give me the impression you understand my problem?

- Are you realistic in your methods and approach?

- Do you agree with my analysis?

- Are you focusing on the right issues?

- Are you projecting confidence?

- Are you making me think differently about the problem?

- How long will this data collection process take?

- How disruptive will the work be to my operation and organization?

- Do you provide me with a sense of urgency?

- Are you adding some new light on the problems?

- Are you listening to me and my concerns?

Other statements/questions you might use:

- Can you tell me a little more about...

- You mentioned earlier... can you say more about that

- Are you sure that x is a real problem?

- How do you know that x caused the problem?

- Can you explain...?

- Could you describe what actually happened...?

- Then what took place?

- Did anyone argue against it?

- But you said this has been going on for many years and nothing has happened, why has this been the case?

- How did that happen?
- Could you outline the strengths of the current situations?
- What are the weaknesses of the current situation?
- Are there any other potential risks?
- If you could do one thing to improve the situation what would it be?

SIX
Managing change

Understanding organizational change

Regardless of the consultancy projects we work on, managing change is always central to them. Whether it be a new MIS system, organization structure or change in operational processes, change of some description has to result. To be a successful internal consultant we need to be able to understand and master the dynamics of organizational change.

In a change process we have to help clients gain a a clear understanding of where they are and where they need to go. Change then involves moving the situation or organization from point A to point B. If the change transition is to be successful we will need to identify a number of core factors and pull a series of 'levers' along the way. This process we refer to as change management.

Figure 23 identifies some of the issues and levers that will need to be managed in most change management processes.

In understanding change we have to focus on two key areas. Firstly, we need to appreciate how individuals react to change and to learn to plan for these reactions in our day-to-day work. Secondly, we need to develop an understanding of the factors that influence organizational change.

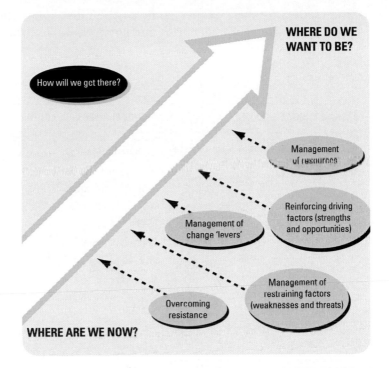

FIGURE 23: MANAGING THE CHANGE

Individual reactions to change

Change and how people react to it is often defined in terms of a series of endings and beginnings. People often have to say goodbye to the past and then come to terms with, or embrace the new. Change can often provoke a sense of shock or loss in people and that is why we need to be prepared for different individual reactions. In major change scenarios this sense of shock can have dramatic consequences for all the parties involved. It might even result in major forms of resistance to the proposed changes as illustrated by temporary work stoppages, strikes or even sabotage.

The following table outlines some of the most common organizational change scenarios and some typical individual reactions that might result.

ORGANIZATIONAL CHANGES	INDIVIDUAL CHANGES – REACTIONS
Merger, acquisition/takeover	• Loss of direction • Ambiguity about what the new situation involves – leading to uncertainty and insecurity • Excitement over the changes and new opportunities • Creation of a 'winners and losers' atmosphere.
New CEO	• New strategies, rules and priorities • Need to develop new relationships – build new credibility • Sense of urgency – need to perform.
Senior Management 'shake-outs'	• Changes in power base and key stakeholders within the organization – individuals having to develop new networks • Loss of power or sense of newly acquired power • New rules and priorities.

ORGANIZATIONAL CHANGES	INDIVIDUAL CHANGES – REACTIONS
Loss of major customers/ market turbulence	• Uncertainty and sense of crisis • Possible redundancies – fear of unemployment.
Changes in capital structure e.g. stock market flotation, acquisition	• Possible change in management style and commitment to the organization. • New owners and performance regime – change in habits.
Privatisation	• Changes in working practices, • Clash of value sets – people may not want to be profit driven.
Rapid growth	• Loss of small company climate – individuals may not like the formality of a bigger organization • Chaos and dis-organization – out of control • Urgent need for new practices, systems and processes • Pressure to keep up.

Woodward and Buckholz in their book 'Aftershock' identified four classic reactions towards change events. These consist of disengagement, dis-identification, dis-orientation and dis-enchantment.

As an internal consultant we can expect to have to deal with all of these reactions at some stage or another. In very complex projects we might have to deal with different groups of people who are at four stages. Central to our consultancy approach is trying to look ahead and predict difficult situations. If we can do this then we can develop contingency plans and actions. Understanding where people might be on these emotional scales will certainly help us to understand the way people are behaving. In any change process emotions play a major role. Failing to recognise and plan for this emotion will result in greater difficulties when we come to implement a change.

1 Dis-engagement

- Loss of initiative and commitment.

- Do as little as possible.

- Withdraw/maintain a low profile.

- Energy lost – survival and self preservation becomes the priority.

- Go to the bunker.

- Quit.

  'Just keep your head down'
  'Don't do anything risky'
  'I'll just do my job from now on'
  'This happens every 2 years'

2 Dis-identification

- Loss of identity.
- 'I used to…'
- I am no longer OK!
- Living in the past.
- Back to the future.

  'It's not fair'
  'They didn't ask me'
  'Why did it have to happen to me?'

3 Dis-orientation

- Feeling of loss and confusion.
- Lost priorities.
- Loss of direction.

  'Now what do I do'
  'What do I need to learn'
  'What is going on'
  'What next?'

4 Dis-enchantment

- What has gone has gone.
- The good old days.
- 'Victim' behaviours.
- Need to enlist support from others.
- Back stabbing.
- Revenge.

  It's just not like it used to be'
  'They won't get anywhere with this'
  'I cannot believe what has happened'
  'They will be sorry'

The change transition curve

Another classic and helpful way of viewing individual reactions to change is to look at it as a series of stages. Adams, Hayes and Hopkins in their work 'Transitions' developed a 'transition curve' approach to change. This analysis is frequently associated with the emotions and grieving process that people experience with the death of a close friend or relative.

Stage 1: Shock and immobilisation

Why me? What have I done to deserve this? How could this have happened?. We are shocked that the change has taken place – 'They have sold the company or announced the closure of the plant – it is unbelievable!' This is a shock reaction – we are immobilised and show an inability to do anything.

Stage 2: Denial and disbelief

This stage involves denial and disbelief that the change has actually happened.

> 'Why did it have to happen to me? It cannot be true.' 'Why them? They did not deserve it!'

In some cases people may even revert to their previous work behaviours. The redundant worker continues to get up to go to work and actually travels to the plant. The executive refuses to inform their family that they have been replaced. The same forms and processes are completed.

Whilst this initial reaction is normal it is of course important that people get help to move into the new scenario.

Stage 3: Incompetence/guilt/depression

Next we begin to understand the new situation but feel incompetent and frustrated by the new order of things.

At this stage we may feel that we cannot cope with the new; that we lack the necessary skills or confidence in ourselves or the new situation. In extreme cases some people might feel guilty that they kept their jobs in the restructuring whilst others were fired. Alternatively, they may feel depressed that they were denied the opportunity to leave with a large pay-off.

Clearly training initiatives and effective communication processes can help people through this very difficult phase.

Stage 4: Accepting reality

At this stage we begin to come to terms with the change and accept the new reality. There maybe a new willingness to try out the new practices and to generally begin moving on.

'I have to move on and just try to get on with it!'

'Well, life has to go on'

Stage 5: Rationalising and testing

At this stage we are really beginning to cope with and manage the new situation or demands being placed upon us. We may also make mistakes and use up a lot of energy in trying to get to grips with the new order. But slowly by trial and error we begin to learn and cope.

Stage 6: The search for meaning and acceptance

At this stage we try to reflect on what has happened to us. We seek to understand what is different and why we became so frustrated or angry about the change. We may begin to share our feelings and views with others as a way of making sense of the whole process.

Stage 7: Internalising the change

The change process and transition has finished and we begin to feel comfortable and confident with the new situation. We have come to adapt and cope with the change and return to a new sense of normality.

The great value of the transition curve is that it again provides a framework for us to understand what is happening to people when they experience major change. By reflecting on the model we can both plan and manage change projects in a more effective and integrated way. The important point to try to gauge is where people might be at a particular point in time on a change project. If we can do this we can again think about developing responses to deal with the reactions.

We obviously need to think about how we trigger various change events and how we are are going to deal with the people issues. There is no point being very excited and optimistic about a change if your client audience is stuck in the first stage of shock and denial. In such cases we will need to develop appropriate strategies to help people move through the various phases in line with our project deliverables.

The transition curve

Understanding the seven phases will speed up the transition process.

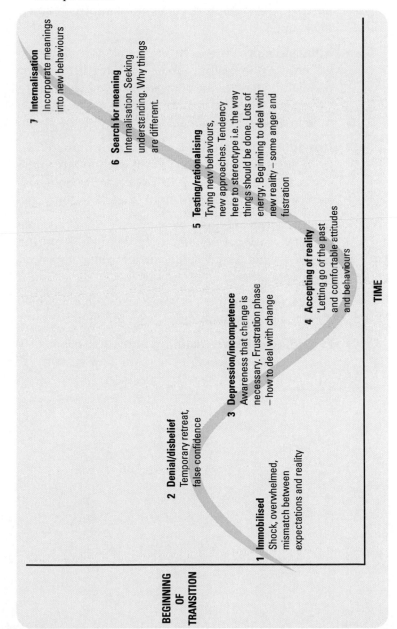

BEGINNING OF TRANSITION

1 Immobilised
Shock, overwhelmed, mismatch between expectations and reality

2 Denial/disbelief
Temporary retreat, false confidence

3 Depression/incompetence
Awareness that change is necessary. Frustration phase – how to deal with change

4 Accepting of reality
'Letting go of the past and comfortable attitudes and behaviours

5 Testing/rationalising
Trying new behaviours, new approaches. Tendency here to stereotype i.e. the way things should be done. Lots of energy. Beginning to deal with new reality – some anger and frustration

6 Search for meaning
Internalisation. Seeking understanding. Why things are different.

7 Internalisation
Incorporate meanings into new behaviours

TIME

Very often we will need to consider a range of possible actions including:

- **Improving the communications and information flow** – to help people become more informed about the change.

- **Allowing more time** – if strong emotions are involved we need to be realistic about the time it takes for people to adjust to the change – so we may have to slow down and build in more time just to allow people time to digest the changes.

- **Providing increased access to senior managers** – in stressful situations people will want to talk to the key players and so it maybe necessary to hold sessions with the top management to address concerns.

- **Incentivising actions** – we may need to help people by showing what benefits they will gain from the change – whether it be financial or through improved work processes or environment.

- **Forcing the change** – in some cases there maybe a need to drive through the change forcefully.

- **Providing access to training and other resources** – to develop their confidence in the new system.

Managing organizational change

As well as understanding how individual's react to change we also need to be able to understand the wider issues that impact on organizational change.

In any change process it is critical to be aware of the wider organizational factors and issues that impact on the likelihood of success or failure.

Experience suggests that any organizational change can generate some of the following issues and problems.

People hold onto the past

As we have already identified, a frequent characteristic of change is that some people prefer to hold onto the past and so resist the introduction of the new.

People revert to type easily

People like to go where they are comfortable. So, even after some initial efforts to change, people will often slip back into their old way of doing things. Rather like the proverbial new year's resolution, people soon lose their enthusiasm for the change if other factors are not also in place.

Skills and knowledge gaps open up

Transition to the new may mean that people need to learn new knowledge or skills in order to adapt to the new order. If efforts to address these gaps are not made then the chances are that the change will impact negatively by a lack of people capability.

Failing to manage the hard or soft issues

In any complex organizational change there is a need to often address both the soft and hard elements of change. There is no point in training people and motivating them if the system they are to operate will not deliver the information necessary to make the customer happy.

Equally, investing heavily in new information systems and equipment will not work if the people who are to operate the new systems are either demotivated or lacking in skills. To achieve effective change you have to manage the hard and the soft elements of change.

The old management is left in place

Frequently, change fails as the old regime is left to manage the change. In achieving and driving through complex change you may well need to consider making changes at the top or with the middle management. You have to ask why were the changes not actioned by the existing management?

We give up too easily

Many change initiatives are not allowed sufficient time to succeed. When faced with a sharp dip in the transition curve of change many managements will give up. Cries of 'it's not going to work' or 'the results are not happening!' can all too easily mean that projects are terminated too early on. When the process becomes difficult you need to show a strong nerve and commitment to follow things through, and not give up at the earliest signs of difficulty.

Narrow 'single issue' management

Failing to address the hard and soft elements of change can lead to faulty implementation, so to can a focusing on one major issue. Thinking the problem is all to do with the system or quality is invariably wrong. Complex change involves different dimensions and when searching for solutions you need to ensure that you don't get locked into one form of diagnosis and solution.

Insight

Lack of senior management commitment

Without doubt one of the biggest problems in engineering successful change is securing consistent and on-going senior management commitment towards the change. Many projects fail because there is no strong leadership commitment to drive the change. Alternativly, the commitment is there at the beginning but soon fades during the life of the project. Without a strong level of senior management commitment change always proves hard to deliver. When the going gets tough you need to be able to access people who have authority to make things happen. We will look at this issue more when we look at Stakeholder Analysis.

Consultant or functionally driven

Whilst this book champions the cause of the internal consultant you should avoid running projects where all the control and direction comes from the consultant or support specialists.

Change has to take root in the organization and the best way to do that is to generate a high level of ownership amongst the people who have to own and live the new changes. From involvement comes ownership, and the best change projects are those owned and driven by the people who ultimately will be responsible for the change on an ongoing basis.

Initiative fatigue

Too many organization chase fads and fashions. The result is lots of cynicism and scepticism about change. Avoid trying to present change as an initiative or an event – sell it as an ongoing process. Avoid too many slogans and an overly programmatic approached. Instead, deal with the specific problem and view change as managing the status-quo rather than some big event.

Poor process management

To manage change successfully you have to address not only the 'what' of change but also the 'how'. Process management is all about managing the 'how 'of change. How will we inform the unions at the same time as the management? How will we build a groundswell of support for the change? How will we run the two systems together during the transition period?

Typically managers are very good at classical planning and that is normally about the 'what needs to be done' of change. Process management is much more about looking at the cross linkages involved in complex change.

Organizational change readiness assessment

Prior to implementing a change carry out a quick organization readiness assessment. This is a very simple but powerful way to gauge how challenging your proposed change might be to implement. It builds on some of the issues we have already outlined.

Figure 24 shows the template and a simple scoring against the criteria will help you to assess the change.

Clearly, if your analysis leads you to conclude that people are likely to view the change as being a possible threat to their job security, or might result in a loss of skills, then you need to start planning in detail how you are going to try and sell and implement the changes.

As a simple template you can again use it with clients to get them thinking about the change process and how the challenges might be overcome. It will certainly help you in getting an overview of the potential complexity and in some cases resistance you might meet.

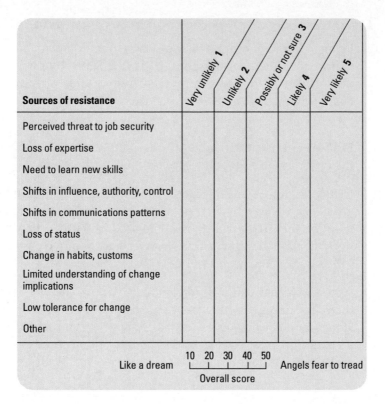

FIGURE 24: ORGANIZATION – CHANGE READINESS ASSESSMENT

Managing organizational change template

Another extremely useful tool to use when planning and managing change projects is the change management template detailed in figure 25.

This simple but very powerful checklist can help identify areas of concern at either the outset or during the lifecycle of a change project. It helps identify some of the critical 'make or break' issues involved in organizational change.

Below are listed some of the key issues and questions that you might need to consider as you score a change project. It is far better to highlight any problems or issues at an early stage than to stumble into them three months into the project.

You can use this template either as part of your project planning process or again as a discussion document with your clients. In a large management group you can ask people to score the checklist individually without discussion. Then collect the scores to collate the overall group results to identify any problem areas. This is a brilliant way to surface any issues involving a lack of common vision or strong management support – which are often critical issues in driving successful change projects.

Typically the checklist cuts across the task management and process issues which as we identified earlier have to be addressed with equal focus.

1 Task Management Issues

- The implementation plan describes the 'What' changes.

- Process issues relate to the 'how's'.

- Process activities enable organizations to make planned changes successfully and to deliver measurable performance improvements.

- Most organizations are good at managing the **what** in implementation but less effective in managing the **how.**

2 Process involves

- Who to involve and in what role.

- Communicating actions, benefits and risks.

- Building, securing and maintaining commitment to change.

- Co-ordinating project activities and packaging work.

- It recognises the impact of culture and peoples' values.

Change management template – the critical success factors

1 Common vision

- Is the client clear about the outcomes and desired end result?

- Has sufficient 'quality' time been spent on developing the end state or vision?

- Do we have the Big Picture clear?

- Is there clarity of the future position?

- Consider workshop/retreat sessions away from day-to-day pressures to address these questions?

2 Unified management

- Is everybody on board and supporting the proposed change?

- Have we adequately discussed and debated the issues?

- Has everyone signed up to the change or is commitment patchy?

- If there is disagreement – Who is raising the conflict – on what issues?

- Can we proceed with the level of support that we currently have?

- Will it sustain in difficult times?

- What are our plans for ensuring we maintain the necessary level of support and commitment?

3 Surfacing of concerns

- Have we provided people with the opportunity to voice concerns or worries about the change?

- Have we made use of staff meetings/surveys/communications channels?

- How have we honestly dealt with such concerns?

- Have people voicing concerns been viewed as demonstrating a lack of commitment or loyalty?

- Have any dissenters been punished for voicing any concerns?

- Have we provided reassurance about their concerns or have they been ignored?

- Do we have a groundswell of support for the change or is there lots of cynicism and inertia?

4 Content management

- Have we a comprehensive plan that recognises the critical issues?

- Are we satisfied that we have thought through all the detailed actions and that nothing has been missed?

- Have we effectively involved all the right people in the planning process?

- Is everyone clear about the plan?

5 Process management

- Have we thought through all the process issues?

- Are we co-ordinating the various elements of the project plan?

- Have we assessed the possible sources of resistance and developed plans to overcome them?

- Are we satisfied that we have spent sufficient time addressing the 'soft' issues?

6 Realistic time-scales and resources

- Are we being rigorous and realistic in our assessment of the time it will take to deliver the change?

- Are we providing sufficient resources to the implementation?

- What contingencies have we put in place in the event of any time or resourcing slippages?

7 Regular and open communications

- Are we satisfied with our communications processes and channels for the project?

- Do we have regular briefings to all key stakeholders built into our plan?

- Are we communicating the plan, it's progress and difficulties in an appropriate and timely manner?

- Are we being open, honest and direct in all of our communications?

- Do we have appropriate feedback mechanisms in place?

8 Systems to support change

- Have we made sure any systems or processes that are involved in the change are also being adjusted to assist the implementation – consider MIS, training, reporting lines etc?

- Are we allowing any systems to maintain the status-quo and thus block the main change?

9 Rewards to support the change

- We need to consider not just financial rewards but others, e.g. the impact on working practices.

- Will effective implementation result in people being penalised for the change in some way or will they be rewarded?

- Remember to achieve change you very often need to pull the financial reward lever to push people along – are we able to do that with the change in question?

10 Commitments honoured

- If we are making any commitments to people concerning the likely outcomes of the change, to what extent are we comfortable that we can honour them?

- Can we deliver on what we are saying or promising?

- If in any doubt – don't. People will not appreciate it and it will make it more difficult to get support the next time

11 Right people in key roles

- Have we put the right/best people on the project?

- If not, will it affect other peoples' views of the seriousness of the plan and the proposed change?

- Will people need to learn new skills? Have we made plans and arrangements so those skills can be acquired

12 Involvement of those affected

- Have people who are to be affected and involved in the change sufficiently informed?

- Remember that from involvement comes commitment! Have we got the right people involved in the planning of the change process?

- Have we left any critical people or groups outside the communications process?

13 Supportive leadership

- What are we doing to maintain the active support and interest of management in the project?

- Have we provided a list of the key actions required of them?

- Are middle management mobilised and fully involved in driving the change?

- How do we propose to secure the continued support of senior management in the project?

- Have we generated the right reporting mechanisms?

14 Measurement

- Have we generated sufficient hard measures to enable a full assessment of the project's success?

- Have we focussed measurement systems on the activities and results we want to see?

- Have we limited the number of performance indicators to track progress?

- Have we advised people that we will be measuring their performance?

- Do we have the systems in place by which we can provide feedback?

- Will there be real pressure to show progress?

15 Effective project management

- Have we ensured key stakeholders have been involved?

- Have we allocated balanced roles and accountabilities?

- Are the key tasks and work packages properly integrated and time sequenced?

- Are the technology inter-faces right?

- Have we anticipated crises?

Success factors	Non-existent	Weak	Adequate	Good	Excellent
Common vision					
Unified management					
Surfacing of concerns					
Content management					
Process management					
Realistic time-scales and resources					
Regular and open communications					
Systems support the change					
'Reward' to support change					
Commitments honoured					
Rights people in key roles					
Involvement of those affected					
Supportive leadership					
Measurement					
Effective project management					

FIGURE 25: MANAGING CHANGE TEMPLATE

Stakeholder Analysis

No review of change management can be complete without a description of stakeholder analysis. We have already stressed how important leadership support and commitment to any change programme is. Very often in organizations, change projects start with a lot of effort, energy and management support but as time moves on and other priorities or difficulties occur, support for the change can begin to fall away. This can have disastrous results for the success of your project.

So a Stakeholder Analysis (see figure 26) enables you to map where the various groups involved with your project might be positioned. It is important to not only carry out a stakeholder analysis at the beginning of a project, but also to update it through it's life-cycle. It is very common for senior managers to lose interest in projects and this is not good for you if a project runs into difficulties. You will need senior management support in tough times as well as the good.

Equally a Stakeholder Analysis can help you and your client appreciate where certain areas of resistance or support might come from. Obviously it is the people who might be out to block a change that have to be watched carefully. But it is equally important to identify those groups who will support the change.

As with a lot of models the Stakeholder Analysis does not provide clear answers. But what they do is help you identify complex and, in some cases, highly political and sensitive problems to your client so that alternative strategies and options can be developed.

When conducting a Stakeholder Analysis consider the following key questions:

- Have we got a strong supporter for the project – High Power and High Concern?

- Do we have any potential change champions – people who will help drive the change – High Concern and Low Power – How can we give them more power?

- Do we have any concerns in the High Power and Low Concern area? Can we push through the change with these people in place? Why do they not support the change? Lack of understanding or totally opposed?

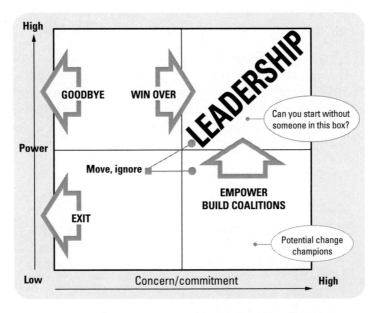

FIGURE 26: STAKEHOLDER ANALYSIS – KEY STRATEGIES

Managing organization change – a checklist of key questions to address

Introduction

The following is a detailed checklist of the key issues and considerations that have to be addressed in any significant change project. Consider using the checklist as a guide when you are planning complex change. Use it with clients to prompt their thinking on the comprehensive nature of change planning. Challenge them if you find their answers lacking. It's better to address difficult issues at the start of the change process than run into them half way through a project.

What is the nature of the change involved?

1 **WHAT IS THE NATURE OF THE CHANGE?**

- Why is it necessary?

- What is wrong with the current situation?

- Can the change be justified?

2 **COMPARED WITH THE PRESENT SITUATION, WHAT ARE THE ADVANTAGE(S) OF THE CHANGE? FROM WHOSE PERSPECTIVE DO ANY ADVANTAGES EMERGE?**

- What are the benefits? For others? For you?

- What other benefits might result from the change?

- Have you considered all the various stakeholders?

3   WHAT ARE THE SHORT/MEDIUM AND LONG-TERM OBJECTIVES YOU WANT TO ACHIEVE?

- Is your success criteria defined in measurable terms?

- Quality: How well?

- Quantity: How much?

- Cost: At what cost?

- Time: How soon?

4   WHEN DO YOU WANT THE CHANGE TO TAKE PLACE? OVER WHAT TIME-SCALES?

- Why over that period of time?

- Do you have any flexibility on the timing?

- Are you certain your not pushing the change too quickly?

- Will your consultations, discussions and communications have been completed in the time allowed?

- Will people be ready for the change when it happens?

5   HAVE YOU CONSIDERED ALL THE DISADVANTAGES RESULTING FROM THE CHANGE?

- What people/stakeholder issues will be involved?

- What may have to be offered to people to drive through the change?

- What contingency planning will be needed?

- How much would it cost if the changes proved unsuccessful?

- What degree of risk is involved compared with the proposed return? Is it acceptable?

- What could happen if people do not co-operate with the changes?

6   **WHAT TRAINING WILL BE REQUIRED BEFORE, DURING AND AFTER THE CHANGE?**

- Will people accept the need for training?

- What type of training will be necessary?

- Can the training be provided internally, or will external resources be required?

- How much will it all cost?

7   **DO YOUR OBJECTIVES REQUIRE REVIEW AS A RESULT OF YOUR ANSWERS TO THE ABOVE QUESTIONS?**

- Would a less radical change effort be more appropriate, realistic and acceptable?

Consulting People

8   **WHY SHOULD PEOPLE ACCEPT THE PROPOSED CHANGE?**

- Have you fully considered the impact of the change from their point of view?

- Have you asked the WIIFM question? 'What's in it for me?

9   **HOW HAVE YOU PLANNED TO COMMUNICATE TO EVERYONE THE REASONS FOR THE CHANGE?**

- Do you plan to provide a thorough background briefing and deal with peoples' real questions and concerns?

11 **IF YOU ARE 'SELLING' CHANGE TO PEOPLE, HOW FAR WILL THE CHANGES REPRESENT A THREAT, BOTH INDIVIDUALLY AND COLLECTIVELY?**

- Do you recognise this may be the critical issue in achieving change?

- How do you plan to deal with the issue of perceived threats?

- Have you identified the key opinion formers and worked on securing their commitment to the change?

- What is the best strategy for persuading or convincing them?

12 IS THE ORGANIZATIONAL CLIMATE RIGHT TO FULLY INVOLVE PEOPLE IN PLANNING THE CHANGE?

- Do you accept there is a close relationship between people involvement and commitment?

- Are you prepared to accept criticism of your preferred approach to planning and managing the change?

- Are you genuinely open to acknowledge different suggestions and ideas? Are you prepared to incorporate them if appropriate?

- Are you clear about your own motives in proposing the change?

- What do you want to personally secure from the changes?

- What will others see you as wanting to get from the change?

Introducing Change

13 WHAT EFFECT HAS THE CONSULTATION PROCESS HAD ON YOUR ORIGINAL PLANS AND OBJECTIVES? DO THEY NEED MODIFICATION?

14 ONCE YOU HAVE REACHED AGREEMENT ON INTRODUCING THE CHANGE, HOW DO YOU PLAN TO MANAGE THE IMPLEMENTATION PROCESS?

- What resources will be required? Will these be sufficient?

- What constraints exist? Are they recognised by everyone concerned?

- Are your contingency plans in place? Can they be brought into effect immediately?

- How will progress towards the change objectives be monitored?

15 DOES EVERYONE KNOW THEIR ROLES AND RESPONSIBILITIES IN THE CHANGE PROCESS?

- Does everyone know who will do what, where, when and how?

16 WHAT EXISTING COMMUNICATION PROCESSES CAN BE USED TO ACCELERATE THE CHANGE? WHAT NEW PROCESSES WILL NEED TO BE ESTABLISHED?

- Are individual and group responsibilities clearly understood?

- Do you have a project team in place?

- What is the composition of the team?

- How are you going to operate as a team?

- How frequently will you meet and report?

17 WHEN THE CHANGES ARE IMPLEMENTED, FOR HOW LONG WILL YOU MONITOR THE NEW SITUATION?

- Who will decide on the monitoring process? Is consultation with other interested parties also required?

- How easy would it be for the situation prior to the change to be able to re-assert itself? What can be done to prevent this from happening?

Reviewing the Change

18 HAVE THE CHANGES IMPROVED THE SITUATION?

- How significant have the benefits been? From whose point of view?

- Have you obtained the views of all those involved?

- Have you achieved your change objectives?

- What other un-intended results has the change(s) produced?

19 DID YOU MANAGE THE CHANGE PROCESS IN THE MOST EFFECTIVE WAY?

- What have you learned about planning, implementing and monitoring change for the next time?

- What have you learnt about yourself and others?

20 WAS THERE APPROPRIATE EMPHASIS ON PEOPLE PROCESSES AS WELL AS THE TASK AND TECHNICAL ISSUES?

- Were all the consequences of the change seen?

The critical questions to ask in change scenarios

1 What is to be changed?

2 Why does it need to be changed?

3 What exactly will be different in the future?

4 When should the change occur?

5 How fast does the change need to be implemented?

6 Will the proposed change really work?

7 Who is supporting the change?

8 Who is against the change?

9 What kind of support can you expect?

10 How will you deal with people against the change?

11 How will the change be communicated?

12 Will everyone understand the need for the change?

13 Is your timing for the change sufficient?

14 Will the change involved continue to be perceived as beneficial?

15 How will you monitor the change process?

16 Will the final outcome be worth the effort?

17 If you were to review the situation again would you still reach the same conclusions?

CHAPTER **SEVEN**

Presenting client feedback

SEVEN
Presenting client feedback

A vital part of the consulting process involves providing your client with continuous feedback on the progress of their project. Being proactive and keeping your client up-to-date concerning developments and problem areas is fundamental. On large and complex projects, client feedback should occur on an almost daily basis. But in every consulting project, regardless of size, there needs to be structured phases of client feedback that follow the key milestones in your project timetable.

When providing a client with feedback you must be operating to the best of your ability. Your client is looking to assess your capability and professionalism. At the same time you will be aiming to secure your client's ongoing commitment to any of your findings or proposals. So it is crucial that the feedback process is managed in a skilled and effective manner. You have to lead your client through a logical analysis and at the same time deal with any issues or problems that might arise. In most cases this demands that you try to pre-empt difficult questions and issues that might be pre-occupying your client. When you manage feedback successfully, your client will not only feel comfortable with the quality of your work but they will also develop greater confidence in working with you.

Of course, when meeting clients on a regular basis you should aim to utilise many of the skills outlined in our interviewing section, but the two formal elements of presenting client feedback involve:

- report writing; and

- making formal presentations.

Both of these activities have to be mastered. In the following sections we provide an essential guide to the do's and don'ts.

Introduction to report writing

Client reports have two fundamental objectives:

- To provide information that significantly informs your client about a particular problem or issue.

- To influence your clients towards a particular view and form of action to solve the problem.

A project report is a major deliverable to a client and they will view reports as major evidence of your ability, professionalism and success in tackling an assignment. The ability to communicate effectively in writing is therefore vital. A well written report supports and promotes your continued involvement in a project. It should also be viewed as a major marketing opportunity.

The advantages of written reports are that they:

- Provide documentary proof of your proposals.

- Are a formal record of your work.

- Can be structured to communicate to different levels of client.

- Impose strong disciplines in planning and structuring your work plan – as well as any final report structure.

- Allow your client time to reflect on your work.

- Focus your client on the critical issues and actions.

- Can be an efficient method of communicating your work to a wider audience.

The disadvantages of reports are they can be:

- Expensive to produce in terms of consulting time and cost.

- Liable to client misinterpretation.

- Abused by clients or others through selective editing or quoting out of context.

- A client substitute for taking real action on a problem – 'We have a review underway!'

- Ineffective unless accompanied by a strong formal consultant presentation.

- Capable off being ignored or not read by clients.

A consultant's report can communicate authority if it is clear and well-structured. Badly written reports can destroy your credibility, your work and your recommendations. A report will only generate an appropriate client response if the original terms of reference have been fully met and you have successfully managed the client's expectations with regard to it's content and structure. An effective client report should therefore describe:

- What you set out to do for the client.

- What you have done in terms of work-plan and analysis.

- What options or actions your client should consider in the future.

- The reasons why your recommendations should be implemented.
- The benefits of your approach and proposals.

A good consultants report will also:

- Provide a permanent record of the work undertaken.
- Avoid misunderstandings (bearing in mind that clients sometimes hear what they want to hear).
- Confirm any client/consultant agreements.
- Clarify major issues.
- Influence your client's thinking.
- Secure client agreement and action.

Insight

An excellent test of the clarity of any report is that it can be understood at a first reading by anyone who does not have a detailed understanding of the project or problems under review.

So give your initial draft reports to someone who has had no involvement in the project and get their reaction. Ask them if it makes sense?

Different types of client report

Persuasive

This type of report is commonly used by consultants when trying to initiate some form of change. It aims to influence and persuade a client to adopt a particular approach or plan.

Instructive

This report advises clients how to do something specific, e.g. to introduce a new system or process, begin an integration plan.

Investigative

The investigative report is fact based and relies heavily on confirmed and validated data to put forward an analysis or report on a problem. For example you might be asked to analyse the results of a survey with no interpretations being attached to the data.

Getting your report structure right

The starting point for structuring your report is to begin with a review of your broad findings, conclusions and recommendations. These areas should define the content of your report. You will then need to consider:

- Dividing your report into major sections of your project, e.g. management reporting, production, IT, etc.

- Reviewing each section in turn. Describing the current situation, key findings, recommended changes and future actions for each section.

- Distinguish between the major and minor points of the key areas. Any minor points are best covered in an appendix to avoid cluttering the main body of your report. Also avoid too much cross-referencing. Aim for a balance between your main text and appendices.

- Present a logical flow in your analysis and link the various sections effectively.

A typical report structure

Introduction

This should cover the background and circumstances surrounding the project. Why it was undertaken. It also need to highlight the key events and client concerns.

Scope of the assignment

This section describes the subject areas under review and highlights any limitations that surrounded the work undertaken. You should list your project timetable, the sources from which you obtained information and detail the response rates to any questionnaires.

Executive summary of conclusions and recommendations

This is the executive summary intended for busy readers who wish to obtain a quick and focused overview of your report. The reader should be able to grasp the essence of your work and proposals by a quick read of this section. It should therefore be written in a bullet point format. Key findings and conclusions should be clearly listed and cross-referenced to any recommendations.

Findings and conclusions

This describes the current position surrounding the problem. It is important not to assume that your client is aware of, or understands the present situation. An unbiased and well-written description of the current situation can be enormously helpful for clients. It often helps to sharpen their thoughts and helps them to focus on the central challenges or problems. List your key findings at the end of this section and make sure you have data to back up your observations.

Keep this section as fact based as possible, prior to developing your conclusions which should flow naturally from the findings.

Options and recommendations

This section should flow from a clear analysis of your conclusions. Once you have detailed your conclusions then develop a range of options to address the problem. This will enable your client to see what scope they have to act on the problem.

Any final recommendations must follow on logically from your conclusions and should contain no flaws in your analysis. Every recommendation must be linked to one or more of your conclusions. In turn you need to provide as much detail as possible in your recommendations.

Implementation plans

It is no good telling a client they need a new system if they have no idea how to go about it. Any implementation section must provide a clear road map to help your client see the way ahead. Recommendations need to state:

- What improvement actions are required.
- Who should take action.

- When improvement action should be taken.

- How long the actions will take to implement.

- What the benefits of the improvements action will be.

- What potential costs are involved.

Future assistance

This is the sales element of your report! It should set out the benefits of your approach and detail how you might assist the client in moving to the next stage.

Closing paragraph

Thank the client and their staff for their co-operation and help during the project. Emphasise your willingness to continue the working relationship and provide further assistance

Appendices

Appendices contain those details and facts that would otherwise clutter the main body and messages of your report. They do however, need to be included as they provide further support for your work and findings.

Writing a client report

When you begin to write a report you will invariably have too much information. A common challenge in writing client reports is therefore the need to be very selective in the final choice of content. Too much detail or an overload of facts may cause confusion. Equally, over lengthy reports that are packed with endless detail are more liable to irritate then actually please your client. Too little and you may create doubt about your whole approach.

To begin writing your report list all the topic areas and data that you consider relevant. Try to do this without judging the suitability of the information. Also, at this stage don't worry about any duplication of data. Once you have listed all the information you can then begin the process of sifting for duplication and eliminating any unnecessary data.

The next step is to begin linking the various pieces of information into themes and topic areas. At this stage you should have a good basis to begin shaping the content of your report. But ensure that you avoid information that is capable of creating client confusion or is based on gossip, or erroneous facts. Only select information and facts that are relevant to and support your main findings, conclusions and recommendations.

Begin the formal writing process by:

- Examining your terms of reference.
- Identifying the areas you are going to focus on.
- Formulating some idea of what your final report structure will look like.

Endeavour to draft or outline the key sections of your report as your project progresses in real time. This will make life a lot easier in the final drafting stage as you will have already prepared some key elements. Always allow plenty of time to write and produce your report, e.g. For a 30 page report allow a minimum of three days and have at the back of your mind that it is more likely to be five days with editing and redrafting. Also allow sufficient time to have the report read and reviewed by your colleagues. It is easy to get too involved when writing and so lose sight of some glaring omissions or errors. A second set of eyes is vital when editing a report.

You also need to:

- Reflect on your client(s) and their colleagues' perspectives on the issues. What are their relative positions in the organization and to what extent do they agree or disagree about the problems? Are they likely to agree to any possible solutions? Are they supportive or hostile? Will anyone you have to report to, already have a biased or negative view?

- Consider whether the eventual readers of your report will have a detailed knowledge of the issues involved? If not, you will need to bring them up-to-date via the report's executive summary and overview.

- Predict and deal with any possible questions that might come from your client.

- Lead your client through the report with a reasoned and logical analysis.

- Deal with any contentious issues in your report by using strong logic and fact based arguments.

- Consider your client's underlying motivation and needs in attempting to solve the problem. Are you really addressing these fundamental points?

- Keep in focus the key decision-maker(s) amongst your client's team.

- Consider any actions or agreements you require from your client. For example, you may want your client's agreement to continue funding additional research or to involve some specialist input. If so, it will be important to highlight compelling reasons for carrying out this additional work, the benefits, timescales and costs that might accrue.

- Find out whether your client will have to sell your proposals to their boss? If so, you need to help your client with this task by focusing on the benefits of your solution.

- Clearly state how your client can action any proposed recommendations.

- Indicate and promote your possible involvement in any additional follow-on work.

- Establish and agree the final distribution of the report.

Other practical tips on writing client reports

- Use plain and simple language throughout your report. Never use a long word where a short word means the same.

- Keep your sentences short. If a sentence works without a word cut it out.

- Try to avoid technical terms and un-necessary jargon. If jargon is required ensure the terms used are defined and explained. If an everyday phrase is available use it instead of any buzz words.

- Use the active tense rather than the passive – '*service levels have been improved*' is preferable to '*an improvement in service levels has been made*'.

- Support your arguments with facts.

- Have clear, logical conclusions and recommendations.

Insight

A very powerful way to build up your report structure is to use the classic discipline of using:

- FINDINGS
- CONCLUSIONS
- RECOMMENDATIONS

Link all your findings to your conclusions and in turn your recommendations to your conclusions. This should enable you to develop a strong logic train. You should not then find yourself in a position where you are presenting recommendations that are not linked to your conclusions or even worse presenting conclusions for which you have no real findings.

You can remember this approach by recalling the following statements:

- *We found...*
- *On the basis of those findings we conclude...*
- *And on the basis of those conclusions we are therefore recommending...*

This should enable you to draw up a strong argument that will withstand your client's review. See Figure 27, *over*.

Remember

If people want to attack you or your recommendations they will look to criticise your analysis. So, if you are recommending actions for which you do not have any findings or conclusions you need to do some more information gathering.

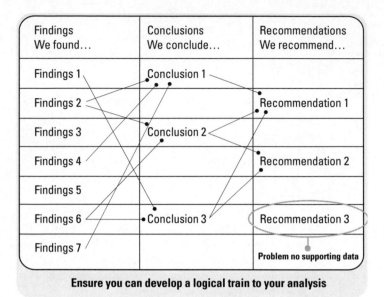

Findings We found...	Conclusions We conclude...	Recommendations We recommend...
Findings 1	Conclusion 1	
Findings 2		Recommendation 1
Findings 3	Conclusion 2	
Findings 4		Recommendation 2
Findings 5		
Findings 6	Conclusion 3	Recommendation 3
Findings 7		Problem no supporting data

Ensure you can develop a logical train to your analysis

FIGURE 27: DEVELOPING A REPORT STRUCTURE

On the logistics side remember to:

- Try to make one person responsible for producing the final report. Reports that are written by committees or groups of people generally prove ineffective and seldom produce results. Collective report writing tends to sanitise any significant points or actions.

- Check the availability of your report writing services and resources. Large reports involve a lot of typing and checking – sometimes through the night!

- Agree when and how you are going to distribute the report to your client.

- Check that your client will be available when the final document is ready.

- Alert your client to any possible delays sooner rather than later.

Reviewing reports

Below are some questions for you to consider when reviewing your report:

- Have we delivered the terms of reference? If not why not?

- Have we described the scope and methods of our work and dealt with any areas we did not cover?

- Are our conclusions clear and unambiguous? Remember that you will have been very closely involved with the assignment. Issues may not be as clear to the reader as they are to you. If in doubt redraft areas that lack clarity.

- Are the recommendations clear and unambiguous? Do they address all of our conclusions?

- Is the report summary consistent with the main body of the report?

- Does the content of each section contain material that is consistent with the heading?

- Is the content, wording and style of the report appropriate to the client's needs?

- Have we used any loose language that might be prone to misunderstanding. Look out for emotive words or phrases as these can always generate strong client reactions. Remove any from your final draft.

- Have we omitted any important issues or facts?

- Have we alerted our client of any possible surprises in advance?

- Who can we get to play 'devil's advocate' in questioning any 'grey areas' in the report?

- Is the tone of our report constructive and positive, or negative and depressing?

Finally, there are some housekeeping points that are always worth checking when reviewing a final report:

- Check the contents page against the main document – are they consistent?

- Check any paragraph and appendix cross-references.

- Check the names and titles of all client personnel.

- Check the section headings and sub-headings; particularly against the contents page.

- Check that all cross-references to diagrams or charts are present and correct.

- Check appendix headings against the contents page.

- Finally ensure that the typing, printing and collation of the final report is also checked. You want to avoid missed pages, duplicated pages, incorrect formats etc. Simple but silly mistakes at this stage can destroy an otherwise excellent piece of work.

Making client presentations

Making presentations is a challenging but essential activity for any internal consultant. We have to be able to present information in a professional and persuasive manner so that the client understands, accepts and actions our proposals and recommendations. As an internal consultant we may have undertaken some high quality research and analysis for six months or more, but all this work will be wasted unless we successfully influence the client and their colleagues in a formal presentation.

As the development of presentation media continues to become more sophisticated so clients are expecting higher standards. Your presentational skills and messages need to exceed your client expectations. It is important to consider that the vast majority of management presentations are remembered more for the presenter than the content. We cannot afford to underestimate this part of our role. We have to be able to plan and conduct dynamic and influential presentations.

Preparing client presentations

When preparing any client presentation consider your client's current position. Are they worried, confident etc? Recognise that the client is important and will want to be respected and acknowledged for their experience. Avoid any patronising comments or observations. Reflect on your client's needs and objectives. Ask yourself how you can satisfy them. Consider the following questions:

- What have we discovered about this problem or issue?
- Have we focused on the real issues? How confident are we?
- Will our findings, proposals and recommendations help the client?
- What are the problems the client needs to address?
- Are we improving the efficiency of their operation?
- Are our recommendations saving or costing the client money?
- What does the client need to do about the issues?
- What other options do they have?
- Are they going to want to continue working with us?

Having addressed these questions, decide on your own objectives for the presentation. You need to consider whether you are asking for your client's agreement or whether you are trying to secure additional resources for the project? These questions will help you to focus further on the structure and detail of your presentation.

In developing the presentation structure make sure that it has three parts:

- A clear **beginning** involving an introduction and background overview to the project.

- A strong **middle** section which details your analysis.

- A sound **conclusion** which comprises a summary and clear suggestions for action.

You also need to consider the overall timing for your presentation and each section within it. Find out well in advance:

- Where the presentation will take place.

- Who will be in the audience.

- How much time you will have.

In deciding on the content of your presentation ask:

- What benefits am I offering my client?

- How do I propose to deal with any difficult or contentious issues?

- How will I involve the client during the presentation?

- What are my client's critical questions/objections likely to be?

- What actions will my client need to take at the end of my presentation?

Insight

Avoid being the expert and talking too much at your client. Always structure your presentation so that your client is invited to comment on your presentation at an early stage. You must get an early reaction to what you are saying. Plan a pause in your presentation after 20-25 minutes and invite client reaction. You don't want to discover at the end of a long presentation that your client totally disagrees with what you have presented.

Early feedback means you can adjust the content sooner rather than later.

Presentation media

In selecting the media to make your presentation you need to address the following questions:

- How do you propose to communicate your key points and messages? (Description, analogy, facts, graphics, examples, competitive data etc.)

- What visual aids or media will best communicate the points you wish to make?

  - PC projection

  - Overhead projector

  - 35 millimetre slides

  - Web-based

  - Flip charts

  - Slide book

  - Practical demonstration

  - DVD/Video

Also consider the room setting that you are going to be using and the logistics involved in employing different forms of media. Remember using complex equipment can increase the chances of technical breakdowns. Also, it is possible that by using overly sophisticated media you lose the clarity of your messages. Many presentations have fallen into disrepair by the over enthusiastic use of the numerous features of Microsoft Powerpoint. So keep any visual approaches in context. What is the key message(s) you want to put across?

Consider the size of client group that will be present? What kind of atmosphere do you want to create – formal, informal, relaxed, sophisticated, authoritative? All these issues involve the process side of your presentation, so consider carefully all these issues. Don't assume that just because you have produced a great analysis and report that is the end of the job. Reports do not sell themselves on their own. You have to influence your clients and this is where your skills in presenting come into play.

Delivering the presentation

Having planned the structure and content of your presentation you then have to do the hard part. Presenting to your client in an authoritative and influential manner is key. As with many of the other skills involved in internal consultancy, we can only develop real expertise in presenting by continuous practice and experience, but below are some of the essential do's and don'ts:

- Make sure you rehearse and practice. Find out if all elements of your presentation work by going through the session in detail. Don't wait to find out on the actual day if your presentation works or not. A serious rehearsal will normally reveal any weak areas in your presentation and provide you with ample opportunity to make any adjustments. If in doubt get a colleague to sit in on the practice session and ask them to be very critical. Fine-tuning at this low risk stage is far better than on the actual day of the presentation.

- Anticipate what questions will be asked – including the obvious, difficult and 'unthinkable'. A key part of your planning is thinking up the really awkward questions that might be asked.

- Stand up straight and project confidence.

- Vary your body posture but don't wander around in a way that will distract your client from what you are saying.

- Avoid fidgeting and the 'classic rattling of coins and keys in your pocket'.

- Speak in a slow but clear and pronounced fashion.

- Smile – it connects with people and says you are pleased to be there.

Insight

Always make your client feel strong rather than weak. Clients do not want to hear that they are either failing or no good. So concentrate on motivating your client. This does not mean avoiding difficult issues but recognise the fact that your client may have been experiencing difficult and challenging circumstances.

Give clients credit wherever possible and avoid slipping into critical or patronising statements. The fact is that in some situations it may indeed look bad but you still have to find something positive to say. Any client that has to listen to a presenter that has nothing positive to say is likely to become an unhappy client. Your job is to make them feel strong!

- Project authority in your voice. A hesitant and mumbling delivery will irritate your audience and destroy your credibility.

  - Vary your sentence length.

  - Vary the pitch, tone and pace of your voice to match your presentation.

  - Use facial expressions that match your presentation content – smile at humour, and try to demonstrate surprise at an important finding or key issue.

  - Use hand gestures to emphasis key points.

- In your introduction provide a brief background to the project and highlight your original terms of reference. This brings everyone up to speed. This is important because you may have some people who are intimately involved with the project and others who are somewhat remote.

- Have a powerful opening statement. A strong reference to the fundamental objectives of the project can be a good way of focusing everyone's attention. Try using for example:

  - *'Before we begin ladies and gentlemen let us just remind ourselves why we are here…'*

  - Following this opening with a hard business issue such as reducing costs or increasing sales will generally get your clients' immediate attention.

- If reporting back on the results of interviews preserve any confidentiality agreements with interviewees by reminding your clients of these assurances. This helps you avoid any pointed questions, such as 'Who said that?' which might come later on in your presentation.

- Speak the language of your business or organization. Do not clutter your presentation with esoteric jargon. Keep it simple, practical and business relevant

- Look directly at all your clients and remember to constantly scan your audience rather than stare at, or focus on, key individuals. There is always a temptation to maintain eye contact with people who are showing positive signs of interest. Remember there are other people present and you should also be trying to gauge their reaction to what you are saying. You need to identify if they seem unhappy or surprised at what you are saying.

- Make sure you summarise before, during and after each key stage of your presentation. If you are working and presenting as a consulting team make sure you introduce each speaker before they begin. We call this 'sign-posting' – it helps tell your client where you are taking them and identifies where they have been.

- Enliven your presentation by the use of appropriate comments or quotes which you recorded during the course of your research. A simple but insightful quote to illustrate some statistical or graphical point can be very powerful. But do remember to safeguard confidentiality of the speaker. If necessary make the quote anonymous except for a generic job title or role description.

Insight

When making a client presentation try to use 'WE' rather than 'YOU'. It is always easy to slip into a telling mode when giving a presentation and bad consultants start saying things like:

- You have some major problems here.
- You need to tackle these issues.
- You must address this problem.

To a client this can sound very irritating and condescending. Remember, we are on the same side so always use 'we' rather than 'you'. It helps develop rapport and sounds significantly better to your client.

Similarly use 'challenges' not 'problems'. Stating that 'we have some major challenges' is far better than saying 'you have some major problems'. Keep the language positive and upbeat.

- Watch for individual client responses as your presentation develops.

  - Nodding heads or frowns should be picked up on by reflecting questions back to the client.

  - 'You seem a little unhappy with that last point? Have we missed something?'

  - 'Is that finding an issue for you Bob?'

- Pace your presentation so that it gathers momentum from beginning to the end.

If you are presenting options to your client use a simple cost benefit approach to focus your client's thoughts. Simply using a high, medium and low rating can add considerably to any subsequent debate and will help develop your client's commitment to any eventual selection decision. Figure 28 illustrates this simple but powerful approach. Proposing options is a classic example of operating in a process rather than an expert mode.

OPTIONS	Cost of implementation	Benefits to organisation	Practicality/ease of implementation
A	HIGH	HIGH	HIGH
B	HIGH	MEDIUM	HIGH
C	LOW	MEDIUM	LOW
D			
E			

FIGURE 28: PRESENTING CLIENT OPTIONS

- Don't 'fade away' at the end of your presentation. Make sure you have a strong and powerful close.

- Allow ample time for discussion at the end of the presentation. Engaging your client is critical so ensure you allow sufficient time to discuss the issues that have been raised.

- Remember to be enthusiastic and confident – if you are not, how can you expect your clients to be?

Presenting client feedback – being client focused

This stage involves you presenting feedback back to your client throughout a project life-cycle. It involves writing reports, making presentations and writing key reports.

Questions you should ask:

- Is your analysis rigorous, accurate and clear?

- Can you support your findings, conclusions and recommendations?

- Will your findings and recommendations help your client?

- Will your client(s) respond positively or negatively to your feedback?

- Have you managed your client's expectations in advance of your feedback presentation?

- Is your feedback presentation in the right format, style and level of detail?

- Have you spent enough time rehearsing for your presentation?

- Have you thought of all the 'unthinkable' questions?

- Have you adequately planned how to move your client forward to the next stage of the project?

- How will you report back to interviewees who helped you during the information gathering phase of your work?

Client's perspective of you:

- How valid is their analysis and feedback?

- How thorough has the research been?

- Have they upset anyone during the work?

- Do I understand, accept and agree with the findings or results?

- How will my colleagues react to your findings and recommendations?

- How well have they managed the feedback process?

- Have they dealt adequately with my questions and concerns?

- Have they added to my understanding of the issues and problems?

- Do the recommendations represent a solution to the problem?

Typical client thoughts and reactions when receiving feedback – have you got the right answers?

- So what conclusions have you produced?
- I can't believe that problem is actually happening.
- I would like to get a quick overview of your findings.
- I would like to spend more time examining this issue.
- Who said that? It's rubbish, it can't be true!
- How have you come to that conclusion?
- You found that people thought…?
- I am startled to be told that…
- Was there anything positive that you discovered?
- It's all pretty bad news.
- Are we doing anything well?
- OK, what do we need to do next?
- I can't help thinking you have missed something there.
- I think you may have misinterpreted that point.
- That cannot be true.
- I tend to agree with that.
- Yes, that is interesting.
- I would like to comment on one key point.

Other statements/questions you might use:

- There were some positive as well as negative issues emerging from our investigation.
- We would like to provide you with an overview of our findings and then focus on some specific issues.

- We are not sure about this specific point, but we think what is happening here is...

- We would welcome your reactions to these points.

- You may disagree, but the results do indicate a strong negative perception about this issue.

- Perhaps we need to get additional information about that question.

- This point is certainly reinforced by section ten of our report.

- We will cover those points later on in our presentation.

- Perhaps I could cover that subject at the end of our presentation.

CHAPTER EIGHT

Implementing, reviewing and
exiting projects

Implementing, reviewing and exiting projects

Project implementation

In implementing any project you will need to be able to plan and manage effectively. The key elements of project planning and implementation involve developing a list of key activities and resources and a time-line for completion. Any project also involves risk, so you will need to review key aspects of your implementation plan and assess any significant risks associated with it.

So, think in terms of project implementation as managing resources, time and quality with a keen eye on any possible risks that might occur. As well as planning the project you will also need to ensure that you both control and lead the project.

Project control is all about measuring, evaluating and correcting progress throughout the life-cycle of the project. Central to this is your project master plan and the need to constantly monitor progress against it.

Figures 29, 30 and 31 detail a draft plan and process for conducting a risk assessment.

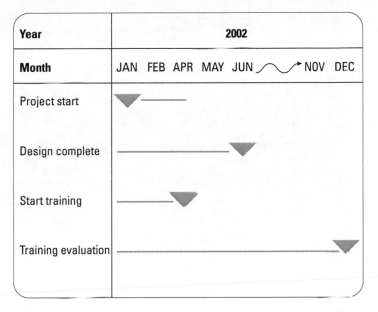

Year	2002							
Month	JAN	FEB	APR	MAY	JUN		NOV	DEC
Project start	▼							
Design complete					▼			
Start training				▼				
Training evaluation								▼

FIGURE 29: PROJECT MASTER PLAN

In conducting a risk assessment you need to consider your overall plan and review each key task against two key questions:

1   The probability of failure associated with that task – what if it did not happen as you have planned?

2   The possible impact it would have on your project – would it severely impact on the implementation plan?

By simply using a high, medium and low rating you can quickly identify parts of your plan that may need some kind of alternative or contingency planning.

As a general rule, if you identify an activity that has a medium probability of failure and a medium impact on the project then you need to develop some alternatives or contingency plans for that activity.

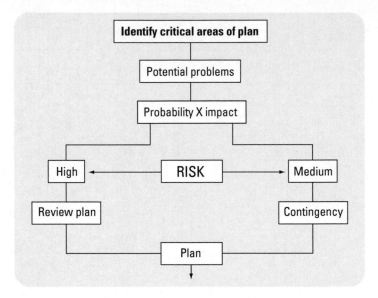

FIGURE 30: RISK ASSESSMENT IN PROJECTS

Task	Probability of failure	Impact on project	Contingency
Delivery of plant	Medium	High	Investigate alternative suppliers

1 Avoid hiding contingency in other tasks.

2 Don't add contingency at the end of phases or project end.

3. Contingency comes from carrying out a risk analysis.

FIGURE 31: RISK ANALYSIS

Obviously there are a lot of other project management techniques that can be used, and those readers who wish to get a more detailed account should read 'Project Skills' (Butterworth Heinemann, 1998) written by Dr Sam Elbeik and myself. In this book we go into the details of project management and the associated skills.

Project implementation – being client focused

This stage of the consulting cycle involves you managing the detailed project implementation.

Questions you should ask:

- Have you secured your client's agreement to the plan?
- Are you confident about your project management skills and capability?
- Have you prepared a briefing pack for the implementation team?
- Have you spoken to each individual team member?
- Will there be any conflicts arising with other parts of the organization as your work develops?
- Have you spent sufficient time thinking about the balance and composition of your team?
- Have you communicated with relevant suppliers and other interested parties?
- Do you have the necessary control and reporting procedures in place?
- Have you agreed regular access to your client during the implementation period?

Client's perspective of you:

- Are you competent?

- Does everything seem to be under control?

- Am I getting regular updates of progress?

- Have I been involved in the important meetings?

- Does it all seem realistic and feasible?

- Are they capable of taking people along with the changes?

Other statements/questions you might use:

- We would welcome your attendance at the launch meetings.

- Perhaps you would be prepared to welcome people and outline your expectations.

- We are experiencing some problems with Department X and would like to discuss it with you before it becomes a big issue.

- Here are the key developments arising out of the last week's work.

- We are still on track.

- How do you think things are progressing?

- What feedback have you received from other people concerning progress?

- We may have to reallocate some people resources for that stage of the plan but we do not foresee any slippage overall.

- We may need to re-negotiate some extra time or resources as a result of last week's problems.

Reviewing consultancy projects
– being client focused

This final stage of the client project involves establishing whether your project's objectives were achieved and formally 'signing off' your involvement in a project.

Questions you might ask:

- Have you signalled the end of the project/assignment earlier with your client, thus avoiding any surprises?
- Have you agreed a project end date with your client?
- Is there to be a formal hand-over of the project to your client?
- Is your client comfortable with the close of the project?
- Are there any major issues still outstanding that are worrying your client?
- Have you secured the views of all the relevant parties?
- Have you been sufficiently rigorous in your review process?
- Have you been open and honest about any problem areas?

Client's perspective of you:

- Have you given me ample notice of the project's conclusion?
- Have you fulfiled the terms of reference?
- Have I enjoyed working with you?
- Would I want to work with you again?
- Have you left a positive impression on my team?
- Were you always open, honest and direct in your dealings?

Other statements/questions you might use:

- We would like to have a final meeting to conclude and review our work.

- Are you happy with everything?

- Are there any outstanding issues?

- We believe that signifies the conclusion of the work-plan and the project itself.

- Is there anything that we did not do that would have helped the project?

- We could do that but it would require us to devote additional resources because the project timetable has been completed.

- We do not have sufficient time resource to take on that additional work load.

- We would be pleased to propose to assist you on that additional work.

- We have enjoyed working on this project with you.

Evaluating consultancy projects

An imprecise science

The achievement of the stated objectives is the principal way in which most assignments will are judged. If a project has been managed correctly and the principles we have outlined in this book been applied, the chances are that a successful outcome will be achieved. However, the complexity of many projects means that no internal consultant should ever claim all the credit or take all the blame for failures. Projects involve people, multi-disciplines and changing business landscapes and priorities. This does not mean that you should avoid attempting to measure the impact or success of what your work. You need to know, as does your client, and any future clients, how your work has contributed to successful results. Without this information, neither you nor your clients will know how to manage similar situations in the future.

So often you will depend heavily, but not totally, on subjective opinion in evaluating your efforts.

Project evaluation – questions for your client

Key questions that your client might reflect on in attempting to evaluate your work are:

1 Has the original problem/opportunity which caused you to involve the internal consultant, been addressed?

2 To what extent do you feel that this is due to the efforts of the internal consultant as opposed to other factors?

3 What specific actions taken by the internal consultant helped you to address the problem/issue?

4 What specific actions by the internal consultant hindered you in addressing the problem/issue?

5 What might the internal consultant have done (but did not do) which might have helped the situation?

6 Would you use the internal consultant to help you address a similar situation in the future?

7 What has the consultant left of their skills in your organization for you or your staff to use in the future?

8 Would you choose to work with the same consultant again in the future?

9 Would you recommend the internal consultant to colleagues with similar problems or issues

10 Would you say your internal consultant has helped you significantly?

**Project evaluation – questions for
the internal consultant**

1 Do I believe the client's problem has been solved or addressed?

2 What could I have done differently to improve the final result?

3 What do my fellow internal consultants feel about the results of my intervention?

4 How do the clients staff regard my involvement?

5 How good is my current relationship with the client?

6 Has my client recommended me to their colleagues?

7 Has my client asked me to do other work for them in the future?

8 Did the assignment or project come in on time and budget?

Summary

The answers to these questions will help to address the evaluation question. In the final analysis the client's perception, be it right or wrong, will be the most important feature in the evaluation process. Only if the client believes that your intervention has helped them, will the evaluation be helpful in gaining you further work. But beware of chasing the Holy Grail. If there are new problems at the top of the client's agenda, they may be uninterested in any kind of post-mortem!

CHAPTER **NINE**

The internal consultant's toolkit

NINE
The internal consultant's toolkit

The consultant's toolkit

Throughout this book we have stressed the need to actively manage your client relationships and made many references to using a number of forms to assist you in this process. On the following pages we have outlined a series of single template forms that you might like to use or adapt to help you in managing your clients and projects. They cover the key elements of our internal consultant management process.

INITIAL CLIENT MEETING FORM

Date / Time	Location

Dept / Name / Present

Meeting Purpose

What is the client reporting structure?	Description of client's operation

What are your clients issues?	Initial thoughts to solve problem

Action	Next meeting date/time/place
	Duration of meeting

TERMS OF REFERENCE FORM

Client Name	Date

Consultant Name	Location

Project Name	Start Date

Background

Objective

Boundary

TERMS OF REFERENCE FORM

Constraints

Assumptions

Reporting

Deliverables and Milestones

TERMS OF REFERENCE FORM

Activity Time Chart For Project:

Activity	Who	Effort	Start	Week 1 2 3 4 5 6 7 8

Estimated Costs

Resource Name: **Rate:**   **Effort:**   **Cost:**

Resource Name: **Rate:**   **Effort:**   **Cost:**

Resource Name: **Rate:**   **Effort:**   **Cost:**

Resource Name: **Rate:**   **Effort:**   **Cost:**

Equipment Name: **Cost:**

Equipment Name: **Cost:**

Expenses: **Cost:**

                                        Total Estimated Costs:

Approved by Client: _____

Date:_____

Organization capability: effectiveness questionnaire • '7s' organization audit

Guidance notes

This questionnaire contains a simple series of statements that utilises the '7s' model of organization analysis. The model originally featured in the best-selling business book 'In Search of Excellence' by Tom Peters and Bob Waterman. It is considered to highlight the features of an effective organization.

You can use this type of questionnaire in organization wide projects where you need to collect views amongst staff. Simply adjust the questions to reflect your particular areas of focus. You can then load the quantitative responses onto a spread-sheet, and use the open-ended questions to help structure your analysis and incorporate into any client presentations or reports.

You will obviously need to add a front coding sheet asking people to fill out some demographic data covering the following subject to the precise circumstances surrounding your project:

- Name
- Role/grade
- Location
- Department
- Length of service

Instructions for questionnaire completion

Consider each statement and indicate how true these are in relation to your views of, and experiences on, the organization.

There are no right or wrong answers. We are simply collecting your honest reactions and the data will be used in a confidential manner. No named comments or data responses will be revealed.

1 Strategy

	Strongly disagree	Disagree	Neither agree or disagree	Agree	Strongly agree
1 Business strategy and plans are well defined.	1	2	3	4	5
2 Strategy and plans are effectively communicated.	1	2	3	4	5
3 There is clarity throughout the organization concerning the corporate mission and vision.	1	2	3	4	5
4 Top management focuses on the medium and long-term as well as short-term issues.	1	2	3	4	5

- What changes do you see that will significantly affect your organization over the next two years?

- Where do you think you need to be in two years' time to remain competitive?

- What do you regard as the key performance criteria for you to measure success against?

- What will have to change in order to achieve that success?

- What will hinder these changes?

2 Structure

		Strongly disagree	Disagree	Neither agree or disagree	Agree	Strongly agree
5	Manpower is at an optimum level.	1	2	3	4	5
6	Resources are organized according to business needs and priorities.	1	2	3	4	5
7	There are a minimum of control and management levels in the organization.	1	2	3	4	5
8	Responsibilities and accountabilities are clear.	1	2	3	4	5
9	Responsibility and authority are well matched.	1	2	3	4	5
10	The organization structure is flexible and responsive to changing needs.	1	2	3	4	5
11	The organization structure is integrated, rather than fragmented and operating in isolated pockets.	1	2	3	4	5

- How well do the different parts of your organization work together?

- How effective is communication vertically within your organization?

- How effective is communication horizontally within your organization?

- What effect does the structure of your organization have upon the effectiveness of your operational efficiency?

- Do people have appropriate levels of authority and responsibility?

3 Style – management

	Strongly disagree	Disagree	Neither agree or disagree	Agree	Strongly agree
12 Management encourages delegation and innovation.	1	2	3	4	5
13 There is an emphasis on coaching rather than telling.	1	2	3	4	5
14 Individual and group achievements are recognised and rewarded.	1	2	3	4	5
15 Performance is measured against clear objectives.	1	2	3	4	5
16 Performance targets are viewed as demanding but achievable.	1	2	3	4	5

- How would you describe the way in which your organization is managed at present?

- How far are you involved in decision-making outside, but affecting, your own area of management responsibility?

- How far should you be involved in decision-making outside, but affecting, your own area of management responsibility?

- How is conflict handled within your organization?

- How far is risk-taking encouraged within your organization?

4 Style – people

	Strongly disagree	Disagree	Neither agree or disagree	Agree	Strongly agree
21 People are valued as individuals and treated with respect.	1	2	3	4	5
22 Peoples' abilities and potential are well understood and developed.	1	2	3	4	5
23 The organization employs high calibre people.	1	2	3	4	5
24 People are used for their strengths, not penalised for their weaknesses.	1	2	3	4	5

- Who are your key people?

- What are their strengths and weaknesses in relation to your organization's goals?

- In what way(s) do you assess these strengths and weaknesses?

- What needs to be done to ensure that your key people have the capabilities to meet your organization's goals?

5 Skills

	Strongly disagree	Disagree	Neither agree or disagree	Agree	Strongly agree
25 Our skills are matched to achieve our business objectives.	1	2	3	4	5
26 Skill gaps are identified and addressed.	1	2	3	4	5
27 Skills are refined, improved and developed to meet changing business needs.	1	2	3	4	5
28 Skills are shared and transferred within the organization.	1	2	3	4	5
• How would you describe the key skills and competences of your organization?	1	2	3	4	5

• How effective do you think these are?

• What skills will the organization need to develop in order to continue to perform effectively over the next two years?

• What contribution do you believe training can make to your organization's performance over the next two years?

6 Systems

	Strongly disagree	Disagree	Neither agree or disagree	Agree	Strongly agree
29 We have effective planning processes.	1	2	3	4	5
30 Tight controls of capital expenditure are present.	1	2	3	4	5
31 Effective budget management is a priority.	1	2	3	4	5
32 Effective procedures for staff performance appraisal exist.	1	2	3	4	5
33 Business and manpower plans are linked and integrated.	1	2	3	4	5
34 There are effective systems for spotting and developing managerial talent.	1	2	3	4	5

- What information do you need from outside your organization that you are not receiving at present?

- How well do these systems work?

- How appropriate are the systems within your organization?

7 Shared Values

	Strongly disagree	Disagree	Neither agree or disagree	Agree	Strongly agree
35 There is a high level of loyalty to the organization.	1	2	3	4	5
36 There is a positive belief in the value of the organization's products and services.	1	2	3	4	5
37 There is a real belief in internal co-operation and collaboration at all levels.	1	2	3	4	5
38 People have a real commitment to values such as continuous improvement, quality and service.	1	2	3	4	5

- What are the underlying values that guide people in the organization?

- What values need to change to ensure future success?

- How do you reinforce the values of the organization among people?

Internal consultant skills
– development needs checklist

Guidelines

- Review the following list of client management skills and behaviours and identify your current performance as an internal consultant.

- There may be some activities not listed that you feel are important, record these in the spaces provided.

- Having completed the checklist, focus on the critical consulting skills and behaviours that you think you need to develop further.

General approach to consulting and client management	I am doing OK	I need to do more	I need to do less
Possessing a strong knowledge base of expertise – constantly updating my knowledge and skill base			
Feeling comfortable with my experience and professional background			
Thinking business first and functional specialist second			
Thinking before I respond to clients			
Being comfortable when working with senior management and others authority figures			

General approach to consulting and client management *(continued)*	I am doing OK	I need to do more	I need to do less
Accepting my client's definition of the problem			
Challenging my client's views, opinions and definition of the problem			
Presenting and selling my ideas effectively			
Working confidently under time pressures			
Promising only what I know I can deliver			
Saying 'no' without guilt or fear			
Enabling clients to use their own strengths and resources			
Helping clients generate solutions to their problems			
Being comfortable with saying 'goodbye' to a client at the end of a project			
Being comfortable with my client taking all the credit for any success			
Being comfortable with clients reviewing my work			
Setting realistic goals for myself and my client			
Using effective project management tools and techniques			

General client management skills	I am doing OK	I need to do more	I need to do less
Actively listening to clients			
Encouraging clients to talk and share their views and thoughts			
Building an atmosphere of openness and trust			
Asking direct and probing questions			
Being brief and concise when speaking			
Stating client problems and objectives clearly			
Developing clearly agreed terms of reference			
Helping clients to own their problems			
Helping clients maintain a logical approach to solving problems and projects			
Challenging my own and the client's assumptions			
Utilising other clients' solutions to solve problems			
Critically evaluating any proposed solutions			
Challenging ineffective solutions			
Using creative problem solving techniques			

General client management skills (continued)	I am doing OK	I need to do more	I need to do less
Reading and interpreting client, group and team dynamics accurately			
Appreciating the impact of my behaviour on clients			
Being aware of my need to compete with others			
Dealing with conflict with colleagues and clients			
Working with people I do not personally like			
Giving into strong client demands – restrictions and limitations			
Being detail focused			
Taking full control and responsibility for projects			
Being flexible when problems and new situations emerge			
Building team spirit in my consulting and any joint consulting/client teams			
Obtaining real feedback on my client presentations			

General client management skills	I am doing OK	I need to do more	I need to do less
Controlling my stress when working on challenging projects			
Intervening with clients at appropriate times			
Intervening with clients without threatening or intimidating them			
Always expecting clients to use my solutions			
Acknowledging failure(s) openly and constructively			
Recognising my prejudices and biases			
Recognising my own defensiveness			
Attributing failure to the client's 'resistance'			
Admitting any errors and mistakes on my part			
Summarising, on a regular basis, client discussions and agreements			
Taking notes, 'writing up' what has been agreed, communicating to the client			
Developing and arranging clear 'next steps' and appropriate follow-up actions on projects			
Using strong project control and evaluation techniques			

What are the critical consulting skills that you want to develop further?

List them below.

_____

_____

_____

_____

_____

- How are you going to ensure that you will develop these skills?

  _____

  _____

- What specific actions do you plan to take?

  _____

  _____

- Write down some actions now!

1 _____

2 _____

3 _____

4 _____

5 _____

6 _____

CONSULTING SKILLS
– CLIENT MEETINGS CHECKLIST

	Observations and notes
Introductions • Role of consultants • Client rapport • Objectives and focused introduction • Timing of meeting	
General client management • Teamwork • Areas covered by each consultant • Control of the meeting – flow, pace • Effective use of time • Active listening skills • Developing client confidence • Success in gaining information • Answering client's questions and issues • Challenging the client's thinking in a non-aggressive manner • Summarising • Re-directing client to other topics • Keeping the client on track • Overall flexibility • Meeting closure • Next steps • Dates for next meeting – follow-up actions • Thanking the client	
Outcomes of meeting • Information gained? • Understanding of situation? • Clarity of consultant's role? • Client's reaction to the consultant? • Overall professionalism? • Levels of confidence? • Teamwork in evidence?	

Success factors in managing change

Success factors	Non-existent	Weak	Adequate	Good	Excellent
Common vision					
Unified management					
Surfacing of concerns					
Content management (The Plan)					
Process management (The How)					
Realistic timescales and resources					
Regular and open communications					
Systems support the change					
'Reward' to support change					
Commitments honoured					
Right people in key roles					
Involvement of those affected					
Supportive leadership					
Measurement					
Effective project management					

Change management action planning sheet

Name: _____ Location: _____ Division: _____

Critical issue definitions	Actions to address	Resource requirements	Timescales	Accountabilities	Other issues

Thorogood publishing

Thorogood publishes a wide range of books, reports, special briefings and psychometric tests. Listed below is a selection of key titles.

Desktop Guides

The marketing strategy desktop guide
Norton Paley • £16.99

The sales manager's desktop guide
Mike Gale and Julian Clay • £16.99

The company director's desktop guide
David Martin • £16.99

The credit controller's desktop guide
Roger Mason • £16.99

The company secretary's desktop guide
Roger Mason • £16.99

The finance and accountancy desktop guide
Ralph Tiffin • £16.99

The commercial engineer's desktop guide
Tim Boyce • £16.99

The training manager's desktop guide
Eddie Davies • £16.99

The PR practitioner's desktop guide
Caroline Black • £16.99

Win new business – the desktop guide
Susan Croft • £16.99

Masters in Management

Mastering business planning and strategy
Paul Elkin • £14.99

Mastering financial management
Stephen Brookson • £14.99

Mastering leadership   *Michael Williams* • £14.99

Mastering negotiations *Eric Evans* • £14.99

Mastering people management *Mark Thomas* • £14.99

Mastering personal and interpersonal skills
Peter Haddon • £14.99

Mastering project management *Cathy Lake* • £14.99

Mastering marketing *Ian Ruskin-Brown* • £16.99

Business Action Pocketbooks

Edited by David Irwin

Building your business pocketbook	£6.99
Developing yourself and your staff pocketbook	£6.99
Finance and profitability pocketbook	£6.99
Managing and employing people pocketbook	£6.99
Sales and marketing pocketbook	£6.99
Managing projects and operations pocketbook	£6.99
Effective business communications pocketbook	£6.99

PR techniques that work *Edited by Jim Dunn* • £6.99

Other titles

The John Adair handbook of management
and leadership *Edited by Neil Thomas* • £24.99

The pension trustee's handbook (3rd edition)
Robin Ellison • £25

Boost your company's profits *Barrie Pearson* • £12.99

Negotiate to succeed *Julie Lewthwaite* • £12.99

The management tool kit *Sultan Kermally* • £10.99

Working smarter *Graham Roberts-Phelps* • £14.99

Test your management skills *Michael Williams* • £15.99

The art of headless chicken management
Elly Brewer and Mark Edwards • £6.99

EMU challenge and change – the implications
for business *John Atkin* • £11.99

Everything you need for an NVQ in management
Julie Lewthwaite • £22.99

Customer relationship management
Graham Roberts-Phelps • £14.99

Sales management and organization *Peter Green* • £10.99

Telephone tactics *Graham Roberts-Phelps* • £10.99

Companies don't succeed people do!
Graham Roberts-Phelps • £12.99

Inspiring leadership *John Adair* • £15.99

The book of ME *Barrie Pearson and Neil Thomas* • £14.99

The complete guide to debt recovery
Roger Mason • £12.99

Janner's complete speechmaker *Greville Janner* • £10.99

Gurus on business strategy *Tony Grundy* • £14.99

Dynamic practice development *Kim Tasso* • £29.99

Successful selling solutions *Julian Clay* • £12.99

High performance consulting skills
Mark Thomas • £14.99

The concise Adair on leadership
edited by Neil Thomas • £9.99

The concise Adair on communication
and presentation skills *edited by Neil Thomas* • £9.99

The concise time management and personal development
John Adair and Melanie Allen • £9.99

Gurus on marketing *Sultan Kermally* • £14.99

Thorogood also has an extensive range of reports and special briefings which are written specifically for professionals wanting expert information.

For a full listing of all Thorogood publications, or to order any title, please call Thorogood Customer Services on 020 7749 4748 or fax on 020 7729 6110. Alternatively view our website at www.thorogoodpublishing.co.uk.